To
Carl
We love you alot.
I still hate oysters, but
I will try other things. We
miss you every time we go passed
your back yard. Love Kelly

The
BIG
FIVE-
Oh!

The

BIG

FIVE-

Oh!

Fearing,
Facing,
and
Fighting
Fifty

Bill Geist

William Morrow and
Company, Inc.
New York

Library of Congress Cataloging-in-Publication Data
has been applied for.

ISBN 0-688-15077-2

Printed in the United States of America

First Edition

1 2 3 4 5 6 7 8 9 10

BOOK DESIGN BY DEBORAH KERNER

For Jody

Acknowledgments

There are countless people I'd like to thank for helping make this book possible, but I can't remember their names right now.

Can you, honey? There's my family, of course. My son, the big fella. And the smaller one, my daughter. And of course my lovely wife . . . honey. You know who you are.

Contents

The
BIG
FIVE-
Oh!

Introduction

"Aging sucks"—Rice University gerontologist Chad Gordon.

Fifty. I really don't want to talk about it. But to help defray the costs—liposuction, relaxed fit jeans, memory loss flash cards, etc.—I will. Briefly. Then I have to lie down.

What were we talking about?

I *had* planned to lie about it, saying I was a mere 45, then going on a birthday-every-18-months schedule until a few million more baby boomers caught up with me so I'd feel better. (Don't forget to lie about your kids' ages, too, or things just won't add up.)

A baby boomer turns 50 every 7½ seconds and there are lots of Pollyannas out there writing books telling you that this is the best time of your life, your second adolescence, your "middessence," your "mid youth," your "Flaming Fifties." They go so far as to redefine "middle age" as 60–75 years old to make you feel better. Fine. (And your ideal weight is eight pounds more than you weigh now. O.K.?) They say you're only as old as you feel. I feel middle-aged. 75.

When that Heaven's Gate cult checked out this year, they said they were "leaving their vehicles"—leaving their bodies behind. That's what I need, a new vehicle. I need to go vehicle shopping. Got anything in a Mel Gibson? Antonio Banderas? Maybe a Demi Moore for the Mrs.?

Baby boomers are not aging gracefully. We're fighting it every step of the way, making the War On Aging a national crusade, dedicating some of our nation's greatest scientific minds and medical talents to developing new forms of cosmetic surgeries, new exercise contraptions, new diets, new miracle fabrics that camouflage and contain, and all manner of expensive new anti-aging ointments.

This book documents my own tussle with 50, from the awful moment I opened my (unsolicited) American Association of Retired Persons (AARP) membership card (sent to almost every American on or about their fiftieth birthdays), to my trips to the tailor to alter my trousers (again), to visiting a New York skin salon and a California "fountain of youth" health spa, to the appointment with the liposuction man, to buy trifocals, to buy a proper mid-life crisis mobile, to a "fun fair" and a new store for the over-50 set, to health clubs, to the Memory Loss Center, to being the oldest guy at the rock concert (except the band), to dropping my kid off at college, to dropping basketball and taking up golf, to dealing with graying hair and libido loss, to attending a meeting of a group of menopausal women named The Red Hot Mamas, to parties where people fall asleep, to visiting the Life Extension Institute and a man who is doing everything known and not quite yet known to science to stay young.

I don't mean to be negative. Oh sure, I have noticed some changes: I can't see anymore; the dermatologist wants me to stop by to remove some basal cell somethings or others; my crow's feet are the size of giant emu tracks; my hair is turning lighter by the hour; my belt is two notches beyond where I thought it would ever be (possibly more, I can't see it right now); I lost my libido around here someplace; I find myself saying "huh?" a lot; I periodically get a stiff neck and sore back; I seem to have permanent tennis elbow; I can't remember names; my energy starts running a little low around noon; and friends my age suggest I take Prozac like they do or this stuff will get me down. I know, I know. I really should see a doctor about all this. But not just any doctor. Doctor Jack Kevorkian.

50 Ways to Tell You're 50

1. Test-drive Cadillac
2. Have to "double pump" to get out of taxicab
3. Longer recovery time between orgasms (six weeks at VA Hospital)
4. Never heard of Grammy winners
5. Make grunting sounds putting on socks
6. Drop Playboy Channel, pick up Food Network
7. Attend menopause awareness seminars to meet chicks (men)
8. Able to periodically defrost Hungry-Man Double Entree TV dinner with bare hands (women)
9. Take three tries to call own kids by correct names
10. Switch from frozen margaritas to Sustacal and vodka
11. Can't read menu
12. Can't hear specials
13. Couldn't remember them even if you could
14. Now play air guitar only to "unplugged" records
15. Can't buy CDs because don't know how to open them
16. Fight with toddlers over last disposable diaper in box
17. Ear hair
18. Aquacize

19. Can't see squat (eyesight's failing)
20. Can't see dick (literally)
21. Mall walk
22. Can't recall last sex act (and there was no second party to ask)
23. Aroused only by buffets
24. Wear name tag as much for yourself as for others
25. Support no-fault farting candidates
26. Canvassers signing you up for organ donor program ask, "Mind if we wait?"
27. Let out pants on the first of every month
28. Can't stay up for Letterman/Leno (and wouldn't know Conan if you saw him on the street)
29. Can't tape them; don't know how
30. Must put some of your birthday candles on *side* of cake
31. Camp overnight at Tower Records for new Tesh release
32. Dig barbershop quartets
33. See withered old codger on street and realize he was one year ahead of you in school
34. Leave turn signal on
35. Forget to zip up
36. Forget to zip down
37. Go to movies you forgot you've already seen (but it doesn't make any difference)
38. Branson vacation
39. Enjoy CBS programming
40. Annual medical checkup beginning to sound like Don Rickles' act (e.g., doctor asks if you'd like a sonogram)
41. Obsessive-compulsive reminiscing
42. "I'd Rather Be Square Dancing" Bumper sticker (on your RV)
43. Habitually "off-line"

44. Clip "get acquainted" coupon for early-bird special
45. Say "Eh?" and "Huh?" a lot
46. New nickname "Twinplex" (ass is getting so big they could show movies on each half)
47. Fall asleep (rather than pass out) at parties
48. Hangovers last longer than three-day flu
49. Have nightmare you're on a bus to Atlantic City with white-haired folks holding complimentary rolls of nickels
50. Stop flipping motorists the bird—and they start flipping it to you

AARP'd

"Ahhhhh!" I scream, slumping to the couch.

My wife, Jody, rushes in and sees me in obvious pain, clutching a letter.

"Is it . . . the phone bill again?" she inquires.

"Worse," I reply. *The* worst, in fact; the worst thing one can receive in the mail, now that a Unabomber suspect has been apprehended and the military has stopped sending out draft-induction letters.

"Who's it from?" she asks.

"Deets," I reply.

"Who?"

"Horace Deets."

"The bursar at Will's [our son's] college?"

"No. Horace B. Deets, executive director of the AARP . . . the American Association of Retired Persons. I'm eligible to join!"

"Ahhhhh!" my wife screams, slumping to the couch.

We all hear a random scream now and then, and what with violent crime dropping and the number of people turning 50 accelerating, chances are the next scream you'll hear will be from someone hearing from Deets:

"Stand back, folks. Give him some air. He's going to be all right. He's not hurt, just aging rapidly, that's all."

"What happened, officer?"

"He was AARP'd."

Another unprovoked AARPing. AARP attack. AARP-related injury. I guess your AARP letter *is* an induction notice of sorts—a notice of induction into old age.

"Like seeing vultures on your telephone wire," as one recent recipient describes it.

"What next?" asks another. "A letter from June Allyson and a free box of Depends?"

Along with lots of "funny" birthday greeting cards on the subject of your turning into an amnesic, decaying, incontinent, doddering old fool, there will come your letter from Deets. I thought I took it pretty well, simply canceling all plans for any sort of birthday celebration and going to bed for three days.

How does he *know*, this Deets? You may not want anyone to know, you may have been able to keep it from your best friends, but somehow Deets knows: you're turning 50.

About one week before my fiftieth birthday the mail arrived and there it was, the AARP letter.

"And I'll bet you screamed 'Ahhhhh!' " said Melinda Halpert, AARP's director of membership development.

"Exactly," I replied.

She said some people call and request that the AARP letter be sent to friends as a practical (cruel) joke.

But it's no joking matter. "Some people get quite angry," Ms. Halpert said. "One woman called and said she didn't want her mailman knowing how old she was. Another woman was living with a younger man who had no idea she was so old until our letter came."

I asked her if this Deets had a sadistic streak. "I've never seen that," Ms. Halpert answered. "He's actually quite nice."

"And you?" I asked, accusatorially. "You're probably not even 50 yet."

"I'm not 50 yet," she admitted. "But believe me I can feel it coming and am very empathetic."

How did they know my birthday?

"Driver's license files, magazine subscriptions, that sort of thing," she said. They get them any way they can. But they get them. Almost every American who's turning 50 gets the letter from Deets.

On his fiftieth birthday, President Clinton said, "I'm going to be all right until I get my AARP card in the mail, and there will be a couple of bad hours there."

President Clinton didn't get one because AARP doesn't send them to government buildings and he lives in one. So Horace Deets gave it to him personally, like a subpoena server. Deets always gets his man.

"We're working on ways to make the letter more palatable," Ms. Halpert said. "We realize turning 50 brings up a lot of complex issues and psychological baggage." (With me it was like the carousel at JFK Airport after three 747s just landed.)

"Our letter to 50-year-olds now begins: 'You're not retired, you're not moving to Florida, you're not old!' "

So why call it an association of "retired" persons?

"We think the American Association of Persons would be a little broad," she explained. She said the age limit used to be 55, was dropped to 50, but probably won't go any lower—hardly necessary with millions of people now turning 50 every year. (There are 33 million members already—about a third in their 50s.) "And you can get an associate membership at any age," Ms. Halpert said. As if . . .

You just send them a check for eight bucks. And you get *what*? A bottle of *cyanide tablets*? Nope. You'll receive (or be eligible for):

- *Modern Maturity* magazine—the largest-circulation magazine in the world, with articles on energetic old people (Springsteen was on the cover!) and products that will help you overcome the litany of aches, pains, leaks, and so on currently besetting your obsolete body.
- enrollment in the AARP pharmacy service (you'll be sick a lot now)
- supplemental group health and hospital insurance (sick and hospitalized a lot now)
- low-cost life insurance (sick, hospitalized, and dead now)
- FTD florist discount (attending a lot of funerals now)
- their pledge that "You're welcome at any one of four thousand local chapters. . . . Meet new friends . . ."

I called Eva Germano, county membership chairperson, to see what was shaking over at my local chapter, AARP Local #3969.

"We have monthly meetings," Eva said, "with speakers from different hospitals and things. It's interesting, but you can't come."

"And why not!?" I snapped indignantly. "I'm 50!"

"You can be a member of national," she explained, "but you can't come to our local meetings until you have applied and we have an opening. Can't get in." I imagined members of the Gray Panthers with Uzis blocking the door.

"We do get openings," she said. "People stop coming. Some die." (Good excuse for missing a meeting.)

"We don't have any people in their 50s," she said. "Our meetings are in the afternoons, when you people are working.'" Eva seemed not too keen on the idea of letting working people— *you people*—into an association of *retired* persons, and she would seem to have a point.

"We've never turned anybody down, but we have to check the application and make sure you're not trying to join *two* chapters. That's illegal." Of course, of course. Can't have people from another chapter coming to listen to *your* hospital speaker. There'd be pandemonium.

I asked her how many members were in the chapter, how many came to a typical meeting.

"Why do you want to know that?" she replied. "I don't know you well enough to tell you that." Jesus, it's like I was asking Eva her cup size. Classified, I guess. Need to know basis. Wouldn't want Saddam Hussein to find out AARP's troop strength in Bergen County.

OK, Eva, OK. Any other activities?

"We did have a six days-five nights bus trip to Quebec last year," she said. I almost asked her how big the bus was but I knew I'd never get it out of her.

Caroline Goffredo, program director of Local #3969, called to tell me that she had the authority to divulge other activities, such as: a speaker on defibrillation; a speaker from the local paramedics' unit; a bus trip to a New Jersey dinner theater; singing; and "I play the piano."

I sat on the couch and read my Deets letter out loud to Jody. "'You have to be 50 to join, but you don't have to be retired,' it says here. See, it comes with a temporary membership card, and, honey, if I join you're automatically a member and you'll get an AARP membership card too!"

"Don't!" she barked. "Don't you dare!"

Losing
Our Minds

Neuropsychiatrists some-
times refer to this distressing mental
affliction as STMLS—"Short-Term Memory Loss Syndrome."

Laymen without benefit of medical training or expertise,
however, often call the malady CRS—"Can't Remember Shit."

There are scientific studies, performed by real researchers
in white lab coats, purporting to show that people over 50 do
not actually suffer much memory loss, that our ability to store
and retrieve information declines just ever so slightly over the
years.

I agree with that conclusion only if "store" and "retrieve"
is defined as writing information down, putting it in a box, and
retrieving it from said box—and providing my wife is around
to tell me where I put the box.

Just such a scientist cautioned me that I should therefore
use the qualifiers "alleged" and "allegedly" when referring to
any *alleged* middle-aged memory loss.

No problem. Now, Mr. Science, could you please tell me
where I put my allegedly lost car f——ing keys? Thank you.

Whether you call it STMLS or CRS, it's bothersome: at

the store, when you can't remember what you came to buy; at work, when you can't remember what you were hired to do; or at home, when you can't remember what you named your child.

The problem is, there is too much to remember these days, too much information arriving too fast. Names, for one thing. I'm in the news business, where we meet many, many new people all the time, and perhaps because we know we'll probably never see them again, we immediately forget their names. This we call "Newsheimer's Disease." We train our brains to flush those names as we move on to meeting a new batch of people the next day. But in this mental process I tend to flush the important names, too.

This becomes problematic at the office Christmas party, where I am well acquainted with everyone there but know only a third of their names. So, I am reduced to cheap trickery, saying, "Have you met my wife?" and waiting for my wife, Jody, to say her name and for them to divulge theirs. This is not a great solution. With even mildly intelligent people I come off as either rude (for not introducing them by name) or retarded (for not remembering their names) or a jerk (for trying to trick them with such an obvious ploy).

You must remember not only lots of names but lots of appointments, errands, addresses, phone numbers.

My telephone number when I was growing up was 2138. To call my office answering machine on a credit card today it's 1-800-321-0288-212-975-4321-830-252-3456-7890-#-5645-123400. And then I hear a message. *If* I'm using the proper phone company. (There was one nice, good, reliable, monopolistic telephone company when I was growing up, which suited me fine and which incidentally gave you a rugged black phone to use that you didn't have to throw away after every call like you do now, but I digress.) Anyway, screw up on one number when you're dialing and you start over.

Remembering to call people back is a problem. You are on the phone, you take a second call on call waiting and say you'll call that person right back, but you forget—sometimes forever. All these technological advances are purportedly to serve humankind. But that's the problem: we're human!

I was told once that if I needed to remember something I should put a rubber band around my wrist to remind me or tie a string on my finger. But, being human, and an aging one, I often can't remember why I put them there in the first place. And besides, wearing twelve rubber bands on each wrist and strings on your fingers cuts off your circulation and marks you the fool, I find.

How bad does it get? Pretty bad. And Jody has just as advanced a case of CRS as I do, so we're of little help to one another. If we saw a murder and had to testify, we'd be jailed as uncooperative witnesses: "I do not recall . . . I do not recall. . . ."

At a cheerful lunch with old friends, questions arise: "When was that, that we went to that great place, you know the place, with those guys, you know who I mean, what's his name and what's her face? Oh, where *was* that? I can't remember why on earth we went there, but it was fun. Wasn't it?

When having lunch with fiftyish companions, try to take along a younger person to fill in the blanks: names, places, current day of the week, month, etc. They're also far more adept at remembering the specials.

In the car, children are good for reminding you—however rudely—to turn off the turn signal and the windshield wipers. And for reminding you of why you are in the car and where you are going.

Questions and more questions. Did we see that play? Have I read that book? Did we see that play? Have I read that book? (Did I write that already?)

Trying to pick the popcorn from beneath the ever-widening gaps in your teeth in the darkness of a theater, there are whispered questions between we two:

"Haven't we seen this film?"

"I don't know yet.

"I think we have."

"Maybe you're right."

"Isn't this the one where the guy . . ."

"Oh God, it is."

"I can't believe this."

"You never can."

"Can we get our money back?"

"On what grounds?"

"Senility."

"No, but we could sneak into the theater next door."

"We may have seen that one, too."

"It's hard to say."

"Let's just stay here."

"I don't remember much of this one anyway."

"Just don't tell me the ending."

"How could I?"

The world is all so fresh and new, and life so endlessly fascinating, when you . . . Can't Remember Shit.

Helpful Hints
& Etiquette Tips
for CRS Sufferers

I have a lot of trouble on social occasions these days, say a cocktail party in my own community, where I'm expected— and reasonably so—to recall dozens of names of people who are known to me, but few of which I can seem to come up with at the moment.

If you're pushing 50 you probably have similar difficulty. So, do what my wife and I do. In the car on the way to the party, we review some of the names of those we'll probably be seeing. We begin with some easy ones, like hers. Jody. And she is married to? Me. Bill.

Artie and Val we have down, as well as Diane and John, Pam and Zeke, Lynn and what's his face. But it's not your best friends you have to call by name. So, it's catch-22. The names you can remember you don't need to, and the ones you can't you do.

I probably should make flash cards to use in the car. My affliction is so severe that there are people I've met a dozen times whose names I simply cannot come up with. If I don't call some of them by name, it's actually OK, because they'd never dream I'm so bad off I can't remember their names.

There is a trick, they tell me, for remembering names: associate a person's name with some characteristic of that person. For example: Sue is a lawyer who *sues* people.

Except that when you have CRS you can't remember what the damned characteristic was. If you can't remember Sue's name, how the hell can you remember that she is a lawyer? You can't. So, what was Sue's characteristic anyway? You grow panicky. Sue mentions in conversation that her husband's name is Jack. Could she be Jill? She is tall. Could her name be Shaquille-a? Maybe, but what are the odds? She dresses like a prostitute. Hortense? And she wears way too much makeup. That's what everybody says about her. That must be it, that must be the key. You go with it:

"Nice to see you again, Tammy Faye."

Sue spins on her heel and walks away.

You move quickly toward the bar. But there's the usual crowd there, including a few guys you definitely ought to know by name but don't. What to say?

There's the old standby for guys, "Hey, coach." "Coach" sort of works, although many recognize this gimmick as a cover-up because they use it too.

A simple "Hey!" greeting can be good. It implies familiarity, at least, along with a degree of enthusiasm for seeing that special friend.

Stringing generic greetings, while slapping someone on the back or pumping his hand enthusiastically, can also be effective: "Heyyyy!" "How ya doin'?" "How's it goin?" "What's up?"

You want to go deeper, to make that person think that you actually do remember him. But danger lurks in these depths.

Does he have children? How many? How old? Boys or girls?

You go generic: "How's the family?"

He tears up and puts his face in his hands. (On the way home, your wife will remind you that his wife just ran off with someone she met on the Internet and that his son is doing three to five at the juvenile correctional facility.)

Make that a double scotch and water, bartender, with a floater.

Guys can greet women friends by substituting saying their names with a peck on the cheek, both cheeks, or a barrage of air kisses. Some air kisses will be unintentional on your part, owing to the woman recoiling and leaping backward to avoid the social kiss, because you may think you've met her but she's never met you in her life.

Occasionally, I'll go out on a limb with someone who looks totally unfamiliar, saying, "I don't believe we've ever actually met"—"actually" being an escape qualifier meaning I may (or may not) have been in your presence before, and may even have talked to you, but without benefit of formal introduction. Or something.

Don't do this, CRS sufferers. My last response to that was: "Sure we have. Three times." (He was polite enough not to add the pronoun "asshole" there at the end.)

You can ask others at the party to help you with names. Hey, they're probably having trouble too. But beware this common pitfall. You pull Ken off to the side and say in a stage whisper, "Ken, is that Ralph Davis we were just talking to?" And Ken responds: "I *am* Ralph Davis."

Avoid saying things like "You have a lovely home here" to the guy mixing drinks. Many people hire help for their parties these days.

Name tags can be helpful, but the wearer invariably notices

your furtive glances, not to mention outright stares. Also, people forget they have name tags on, and women sometimes think you're staring at their breasts. (Sometimes, of course, you are.)

Alas, with our eyes going on us, we often can't read the writing on name tags anyway. Be aware that name tags often have the preprinted "Hello" on them. Remembering this will save you the embarrassment of calling all the women at the function "Helen." And no one's name is "Polo." That's a logo, not a name tag.

Anyway, you can't always employ name tags. I'm told that, unfortunately, they're inappropriate at more intimate gatherings and that I have to stop using them at Thanksgiving dinner.

A Brief History of My Gut

Men, do you ever find yourselves in the shower singing that old Paul Anka favorite, "Having My Baby"?

"Middle age" is a troubling time, not only because your children begin to disappear from sight, but because your genitals do too. For men it's an alarming thing to watch them sinking over the horizon, setting in the South. I mean, is your gut growing or are your organs shrinking—or both? Indeed, are they still there? At the same time you lose sight of them, you're also losing feeling. In most cases (outside the immediate Bobbitt family), they're still down there somewhere. But if it gives you some peace of mind, by all means buy yourself one of those long-handled dentist's mirrors and check.

How did this happen? I was always too skinny. At age 16, I lied about my weight, adding 10 pounds, so my driver's license would read 160, and the girls and the state troopers who saw it would stop snickering at me. I was 6 feet tall.

Back then, some of my skinny friends lifted weights and drank big cans of Weight On— *those* were the days!—which they ordered from Charles Atlas ads in the comic books. Charles was always trying to get all the guys to drink that stuff and lift weights so we wouldn't get sand kicked in our faces at the beach. I'd look at those ads and mutter: "Screw you, Chuck, I won't go to the f——ing beach." (Not that difficult when you live in Illinois.)

I was running cross-country with the other guys too skinny for football, and wrestling in the 127-pound class—so I wouldn't get my butt kicked by those brawny 133 pounders. (The coach had suggested I start wearing sunglasses to cut down on the glare from the lights when I was getting pinned.)

Wrestlers knew how to lose weight. We ran it off, steamed it off, blew it off. Our wrestling coach pioneered in the invention and development of eating disorders. You may have heard of him: Steve Bulimia? He was aided in this endeavor by our school's food service personnel. We always made our weight limits on Wednesdays, for example, the day they served Hawaiian Pineapple Meat Loaf Surprise in the cafeteria. You never knew where you'd see it later.

The rest is history; the history of the ever-expanding universe of my gut. Off-season in high school, my waist swelled to 30 inches. My weight went up to a legitimate 160 by college graduation, but when I returned home from military service, I had dropped to 142 and looked like a Somalian runway model.

When I tell people that these days, they think it's cool and are eager to find out how I did it. Here's my Army diet secret: 1. chain-smoking; 2. malaria pills as powerful individually as a jar of Ex-Lax and 3. plenty of just plain bad food. One actual military field ration was cold, watery, instant scrambled eggs complemented by lima beans.

A few actually ate the stuff, but even then there was simply no time for any of it to stick to your bones. The big, orange malaria pills we were taking shortened the digestive cycle to an average of one minute and thirteen seconds. This made military strategy simple for the Vietcong, allowing them to keep their rockets and mortars trained on sites of massive U.S. troop concentrations—the latrines.

So, my jeans were about a 28 waist, which was the waist size of my tuxedo when I got out of the Army and was married. At 142 pounds I didn't show up in a lot of my wedding pictures.

By age 30, my waist had increased to 32. I kind of liked 32. Felt more like a real man, a little more burly.

By 40, the waist was 34 and I promised myself I'd never let it get beyond that.

But by age 45, pain became a factor. Sitting down, difficult. Laundering, out of the question.

My pants came back from the cleaners a bit smaller each time. The shrinkage is remarkable. We complained to the cleaner, who finally suggested that maybe I was just getting . . . fatter . . . so we switched to a Chinese laundry, where we can't understand their insults.

Dr. Octavio Bessa Jr., of Stamford, Connecticut, recently wrote in a journal of the American Medical Association that many of his patients who were complaining of abdominal discomfort, distension, heartburn, and frequent eructations (belches), and who had already undergone inconclusive gastroscopies and tomographic scans, were found to be suffering from "Tight Pants Syndrome." Dr. Bessa found a normal discrepancy of three inches or more between pants size and abdominal girth and claims 90 percent of middle-aged men suffer from some measure of TPS.

I had that. I had gained 40 pounds since my army days, which was like walking around with a good-sized child dangling from your neck. But I steadfastly refused to buy pants with a 36 waist, which was tantamount to a pregnant woman refusing to give in to maternity wear. A woman pregnant with octuplets.

I noticed that on airplanes I always had to lengthen—never shorten—the seat belt from the guy before me. Putting on socks became a chore.

But I felt I had to stand fast at 34 or risk taking on the appearance of an old boss of mine whose unsightly figure resembled a pear—especially when he wore the lime-green leisure suit. Or the big-bellied neighbor who used to take shirtless summer strolls, causing us to refer to him as "The Great White." I was becoming just such a specimen.

My refusal to broach the thirty-sixth parallel was great in theory, but in reality all hell was breaking loose. Buttons popped. Metal waist clasps on my pants bent and tore free from their moorings.

I got into leatherwork, taking my 34-inch belts—veritable boa constrictors, they were—to the basement workbench and punching extra holes in them with hammer and nail.

Not just the length of my belt but its *shape* began to concern me. When I took it off I noticed it was no longer straight but now had taken on strange bends and turns, like a road seeking the best route through mountainous terrain.

I once found it necessary to unbutton my pants in the car. I avoided doing this at work, however, because another guy does it and forgets. And when the laughter subsides the sexual harassment suits will start flying.

I was forced to seek compromise. Men's trousers don't usually come in odd-numbered waist sizes, so I decided to take my distended 34s to the tailor to turn them into 35s.

He measured my waist and raised his eyebrows, maintaining that diplomatic silence all tailors must.

"OK, 35 and ½," I conceded.

"Certainly" was all he said. A lesser man might have muttered "fatboy," but he didn't.

With each passing year, the swelling around my midsection became more pronounced. "Bees," I explained. "Whole hive."

When we bought our new car, the salesman spoke of the driver's-side air bag. I told him it really wasn't necessary.

It didn't help that, meanwhile, all of my friends were getting even fatter than I was. Some of them seemed almost proud, one contending that his belly represented a monument to Anheuser-Busch, another saying his represented a lifetime of culinary delights. (He drooled ever so slightly, as he recounted favorites.)

One particularly heavy one watches TV from his La-Z-Boy, and in the full-recline position I don't believe he can see the screen because his belly is in the way. I think that's why his TV is sitting on top of two books. If true, it's a fine system, allowing the ballooning viewer to simply keep adding books.

At social functions I'd ask the few friends who had remained somewhat trim how they managed it, and they'd respond with answers like, "I run five miles every morning," which is not what I wanted to hear.

"*Interesting*," I'd reply, taking a pull on my (fourth) hearty ale and licking the warm crab-cheese-artichoke dip from the back of my hand and my shirt cuff. I noticed that often the thinnest people at these parties were sipping Perrier or a mild liquid laxative or something else nonalcoholic and nonfattening—except at my house, where partygoers asking for water are directed to the cat bowl.

Cocktail parties are really the only kind I can attend anymore. When your pants are too tight you can either sit or eat, but not both at the same time. At sit-down dinners I just push the food around on my plate, then hit the 24-hour Burger King drive-thru window on the way home.

My potbellied friends were always saying: "You're lucky. You don't have to worry about your weight." Oh, but I *did*. The long-sweater thing wasn't really working anymore. I worried that it was becoming increasingly obvious what my long sweaters were all about—concealment—especially at summer barbecues.

When I couldn't hold out another millimeter, I made the big move. 36! And went on Prozac.

The added room felt good for a couple of months, and then, possibly due to Sam Lee's faulty dry-cleaning procedures, the 36s themselves started feeling . . . snug.

I'd already thrown my self-esteem to the winds when I bought the 36s—and now *they* were turning on me.

So it was back to the tailor, a different tailor this time, a tailor who wouldn't smirk or raise his eyebrows, perhaps a tailor with no eyebrows at all, a discreet tailor, a mute tailor if I could find one, in any case a tailor from another town.

For 37s! Isn't *Brando* a 37?

Jeans Jam
at the Credibility Gap

*S*norting and grunting, kick-ing and banging emanate from the stalls.

"Goddamnit!" Cursing, too. For these are not horses—Mister Ed never talked like that—but humans, trying with all their might to make forcible entry into stiff pairs of new blue jeans in dressing-room stalls at the Gap.

"Jesus Christ!" yells the same customer, having stopped using the Lord's name in vain and now beseeching Him to come-on-down and perform the absolute miracle of cramming her middle-aged, "Baggy Fit" self into a pair of sleek "Classic Fit" jeans. And the Second Coming is about what it was going to take.

Trying on clothes at this age can certainly piss a person off, no doubt about it.

"We get used to it," says a store clerk, referring to all the ruckus. The clerk is policing the dressing area, picking up piles of blue denims left behind by disillusioned customers. She confides, "One time at another store somebody punched a hole in the wall."

There are no mirrors in the stalls and firearms are strictly prohibited. The combination could prove deadly where "middle-aged" customers are concerned. It occurs to me that the security guard may not be stationed at the front door to control shoplifting after all, but rather to prevent shooting sprees.

DATELINE, THE GAP, PARAMUS, N.J.—"MIDDLE-AGED JEANS SHOPPER KILLS TWELVE! WITNESS DESCRIBES SHOOTER AS 'CHUBBY, DISGRUNTLED' "

"JOHNNY COCHRAN TO DEFEND TROUSER TRIGGERMAN!"

"COCHRAN WINS CHANGE OF VENUE—TRIAL MOVED TO WEIGHT WATCHERS SALON"

"FAT JURY SELECTED"

"RICHARD SIMMONS, EXPERT WITNESS, TEARFULLY TESTIFIES FOR DEFENSE"

"JOHNNY C. TO JURY: 'IF THE JEANS DON'T FIT, YOU GOT TO ACQUIT!' "

"JURY OF PUDGY PEERS SETS SLACKS SLAYER FREE!"

The entire nation suffers from the aforementioned TPS (Tight Pants Syndrome), but I was further suffering from what I call LHOS—Lee Harvey Oswald Syndrome. Every time I sat down in my blue jeans, that steel button at the waist gave me the painful feeling of having just been shot in the stomach by a slug from Jack Ruby.

I had to have new jeans, which is not exactly a desperate situation in America in the nineties. Russia, yes. America, no. At the Gap, I walked into a dizzying array of choices: blue jeans, black jeans, stone-washed jeans, antiqued jeans, weathered jeans, sandblasted and extra-sandblasted jeans. (A guy I know named Alligator Ed blasts holes in jeans with a shotgun and sells them that way for an extra charge.)

I'm an old-fashioned guy—I guess from now on I should say that I'm simply an *old* guy—who doesn't really like a lot of choices. I would like a glass of water, thank you: tap water, not kiwi-flavored water from New Zealand or water with a polar bear and an iceberg on the label that's actually from the Hackensack River. I would like a beer, a Bud, and no thanks, not your very own microbrewed raspberry wheat beer (made at the Bud factory). And, I'll have a cup of black coffee—and definitely not a triple half-caf, half-decaf, almond machiatto. Asshole.

You ask for a cuppa joe these days and the waiter asks you so many questions you feel like you're being grilled by the boys down at the 14th Precinct: "Espresso? Cappuccino? Latte? Single, double, or triple? Caf or decaf? Sugar or sweetener? Cream, milk, skim milk, or nondairy?" It's enough to give you a headache. "Aspirin? Bufferin? Excedrin? Tylenol? Nuprin? Advil? Motrin? Gel-caps? Caps? Tablets? Extra-strength? PM? Give me anything, but don't give me a choice.

I was going on a dude ranch vacation—Yippee-I-Ki-Ay!— and was told I'd need two pairs of jeans, one smelly pair for horseback riding and a somewhat cleaner pair for formal evening wear. Being a traditional guy, I decided on the medium blue blue jeans, but then discovered: it's not that easy, pal! For men they come in "Slim Fit," "Easy Fit," "Loose Fit," "Relaxed Fit," and "Baggy Fit."

What to do? It was like being back in that quaint little Paris restaurant and discovering that no one spoke any English and the menu was in *French*, for chrissake! There, I wiggled my nose and hopped my two fingers across the table to indicate we wanted their famous rabbit dish, but got the frog legs.

At the Gap, an interpreter, a blue jeans somelier of sorts, was summoned, who first explained to me that "Slim Fit" meant a "low waist and a straight leg" and then quickly moved on, letting me know, in as subtle a fashion as he could, that "Slim Fit" I was not. Other similarly perplexed shoppers gathered to listen in. The store really needs a little theater with an introductory slide presentation or something.

The next category, he noted, was "Easy Fit," which he said gave the wearer "extra room," but with a slightly tapered leg. This sounded good, since of late I need "extra room," but my legs are still thin.

A lot of middle-aged men are built this way, giving us the appearance of pears on Popsicle sticks.

I'd hoped our jeans facilitator would look kindly upon me and stop there, but he forged ahead with explanations of the "Loose Fit" jeans, which he said were for their fat-assed, bloated-thighs clientele—or words to that effect. Then there were the "Relaxed Fit"'s, for those who are fat all the way down; and finally the "Baggy Fit"'s for the very fattest of asses and most bloated of thighs among us—but still with legs thin enough they might splinter under the weight at any moment.

I couldn't remember all that (I'm 50!)—especially since he did eschew plainly understood terms like "fat assed" for euphemisms like "those fuller from hip to ankle"—in much the same way a somelier describes a wine as "modest" and "affordable," rather than saying it's "a cheap buzz."

Thankfully, he offered a jeans list that looked much like a wine list. There was a separate list for women, which I thought employed a bit kinder, gentler, sometimes euphemistically perplexing phraseology, like *"Reverse Fit."* Meaning what? A slim waist and extra-thick ankles? No, "Reverse Fit" translates into jeans with enough room for the Twinplex Ass, or one big enough for the showing of two movies simultaneously on the split screen. People who wear "Reverse Fit" really ought to make a beeping sound when they back up.

I thanked the clerk for his help, letting him move on so he wouldn't be around when I made my selections. I didn't want him bellowing: "Let me find you the Baggy Fits in a forty-four!" That type of thing.

Designers for men haven't learned the secret of putting smaller-size labels in larger garments the way they have for women.

"Still a size eight, Bertha," chirps a smiling clerk at the Credibility Gap, a New Store for Today's Fatter America. "I love shopping here," Bertha coos, as smiling clerks open both glass doors for her exit.

I was looking for jeans that would make me look thin, but that I could still sit down in. Otherwise how do you tie your shoes? You have to sit down to tie your shoes, and you can't tie your shoes until you put on your pants. That's why I wear loafers.

I hate the look of jeans with a lot of extra material flapping around in the rear, so, against all odds I optimistically pulled out a pair of "Slim Fit" size 36, then pairs of "Easy Fit," "Loose Fit," and "Relaxed Fit"—all size 36. And, one pair of "Easy Fit" . . . 38s! . . . which I slipped under the pile before repairing to the dressing room, that wailing wall of fashion where there was great moaning and gnashing of teeth.

The clerk said that just the day before she'd seen a set of bejeaned legs projecting from one stall, the legs of a woman lying on her back on the floor, sucking wind and attempting . . . to . . . snap . . . her . . . freaking . . . jeans.

All of my selections did snap, albeit uncomfortably. In the "Slim Fit"s, however, my testicles felt as though they were held in Vise-Grip pliers—a side effect not mentioned on any warning tag. All-in-all the Slims felt like the Lorena Bobbitt Signature Series.

The "Easy Fit"'s offered immediate relief, except in the waist. The "Loose" and "Relaxed" left extra material flapping in the rear, which is totally uncool. Men's legs and butts are often the last to go, so it's important to accentuate them—much as women do their breasts. Some aging men actually have their butts vanish altogether, which is not really flattering either.

As I removed the last of the 36s, I noticed a vicious red mark on my stomach that made it appear as though I had attempted hara-kiri with a butter knife.

So, reluctantly, I turned my attention to the 38s. I took them in hand, contemplated them, then did that which I said I would never do: behind closed doors, I slipped on size 38s.

And it was good.

I tore off the tags. (Levis still carry the size displayed on a permanent leather patch on the *outside*—and wonder why they're losing market share.)

I walked out of the dressing room, leaving the 36s behind, but vowing to return to them someday. Sure.

I walked toward the register, but there were other customers waiting there, so I ducked into the socks aisle and feigned interest in argyles while waiting for the coast to clear. Then I moved forward and placed the jeans on the counter.

The attractive, twentyish clerk with a bare midriff looked them over. "Weren't there any tags on these?" she asked. "No," I lied. "They're Easy Fits," I said without hesitation, pleased to be in only the Gap's second tier of fatness. She kept looking for tags. "Thirty length," I said, a bit more softly, knowing my legs really should be longer.

"Thirty what?" she asked. And suddenly this nice young

woman looked to me like a well-groomed, overly cleanly, frighteningly fit brown-shirt interrogator. I hated her and her . . . slim . . . kind. Probably a size twenty-eight Classic Fit with a nasty chronic eating disorder.

"Eight," I said, almost in a whisper.

"Eight?" she asked, rather too loudly. "Thirty-eight?"

I nodded in the affirmative, looking around to see if anyone was listening, and feeling like some would-be deceiver Perry Mason had just cracked on the stand.

I felt my cheeks turning warm. I was worried she might next inform me about Thursday night meetings of some Fat Man's Jeans club or something. Not to mention the dreaded AARP discount!

Sucking
It Up

Maybe *surgery* is the answer. Elective, cosmetic, aesthetic, plastic surgery.

To hell with all this diet and exercise, struggle and sacrifice. Hoover me!

I make an appointment with a liposuction specialist. A block from his office I start looking around to see if there are any fellow motorists around who know me. I wouldn't want them to see me, not here, not now, turning into the parking lot of a plastic surgeon's office. Why didn't I go to another town? There's one in New Jersey who advertises that he's an "artist." But what school? Abstract expressionist? Would you really want a Jackson Pollock face?

I get out of the car, slowly, checking out everyone in the lot. So far, so good. This is more nerve-racking than when . . . than when this . . . other person . . . this other guy I knew . . . had . . . VD . . . in college . . . and had to see a doctor. I would imagine.

Oh, no, there's a group of people waiting for the elevator! I should have worn a disguise. Fake nose and glasses. Of course I could be here because I'm actually sick. There are other doctors, real doctors in this building. Doctors who are still into that whole *healing* thing. These people at the elevator have no way of knowing that I'm here to see a doctor because my belt's too tight! Riding up on the elevator, I cough to throw them off.

Getting off the elevator, I walk down the hall looking for the right office. There it is, but there's a woman in the hallway behind me, so I walk right by the plastic surgeon's office, then double back after she's gone. I dart into the office and it hits me that the worst may not be over, that there may be people I know sitting right there in the waiting room, where they'd have me dead to rights. And I, them.

Luckily, there's just this one woman in the waiting room, who looks up from her *Glamour* magazine. We've never seen each other and we both smile, smiles of relief.

The receptionist hands me forms to fill out, then a nurse asks: "Mr. Geist, why are you here?"

What to say? I wanted to answer "broken arm," but at the cosmetic surgeon's office why you are there is not so much a medical question as it is a cosmic one. Unless you're, like, the Elephant Man or something.

I dunno, maybe I'm here because I have low self-esteem stemming from a mother with an inferiority complex because of a sister who was an all-around genius and . . . but I don't think the nurse really wants that much information, so I reply: "Checkup." Not good enough. Blank stares, indicating "Insufficient Data Received." I guess a regular checkup at a plastic surgeon's office would be, what? To see if you'd become any *uglier* in the past year?

I tried again: "I'm here for an examination." I think they could tell they had an uncooperative respondent on their hands and had no further questions.

The forms asked all the usual stuff. I was worried you'd

have to give a cosmetic history: of any childhood homeliness you'd experienced; specific dates when you were especially unattractive; if you were taking any prescription drugs for unsightliness—that type of thing.

The scariest form was the one that pretty much flatly stated that your insurance company ain't gonna pay for this malarkey, you're on your own.

The woman in waiting and I exchanged glances, each wondering what the other was in for. She looked normal enough. Probably just a mild case of spider veins, but who knows? She could be sitting on a monstrous ass of operable proportions.

The wait was extensive, of course, so I read all the brochures: Collagen Replacement Therapy (you mean I once had some?); Forehead-lift; Face-lift; Eyelid Surgery; Surgery of the Abdomen; Surgery of the Nose; Leg Vein Treatment; Breast Reduction (now for men, too); and Breast Augmentation.

I wondered if they saved materials from reductions for use in the augmentations. You know what they say: a good plastic surgeon never throws anything away. And where does all the fat go? Does a tanker truck come here every Tuesday and haul it all away? And to where? Tell me it isn't the Parkay factory.

The liposuction brochure said the procedure can be performed on the chin, neck, cheeks, upper arms, above the breasts, abdomen, buttocks, hips, thighs, knees, calves, and ankles. (But they'd probably have to stop and empty the bag.) Can you imagine? You'd come out of there weighing forty-five pounds. It scared me a little. What if, in the middle of a liposuckotomy (or whatever) the doctor took an interesting phone call and momentarily forgot what he was doing? It's happened to me making tomato soup. The brochure warned that there could be "complications," such as "asymmetry," which also worried me some. I wouldn't want to be fat on just one side.

They finally called my name and the nurse ushered me into an examining room, where she tried to pin me down: "Why, exactly, are you here to see the doctor?" I recognized that name, rank, and serial number would no longer suffice. "Stomach," I answered. She nodded and closed the door. Nodded? In agreement? Why that little . . .

I read a breezy brochure on melanoma while waiting for the doctor, who finally appeared in a white lab coat. This was good. I was worried that a plastic surgeon might wear plaid.

It is a little-known fact that damned near anybody, anyplace can do liposuction. Not if you're a Certified, Bonded Housecleaner with a Hoover—not yet. And not at the car wash during "Phase I—Complete Vacuuming," but damned near. You have to be a doctor to perform liposuction, but you don't have to be a specialist and you don't have to have any surgical training or anything. I believe you could be an ophthalmologist, who could do it right there in the office while the patient was looking at the eye chart. "New Glasses, New Gut, in Just One Hour!"

"What's bothering you?" the doctor asked, explaining later that this is the way he has to approach cosmetic patients—yes, *patients*—because aesthetics are subjective. You can't just give an overall evaluation and estimate for repairs. If I were a car he probably would have totaled me out.

He doesn't just want to start in on you: "Gee, that's some honker of a nose you've got there!"

Sometimes patients will surprise him by saying their eyes are the problem when he's thinking "What about that *nose?*" He has patients who bring in pictures of people they want to look like. He discourages this. And sometimes near-perfect specimens come in who are just totally neurotic about their looks, and he'll give them a little pep talk and send them home.

Sometimes downsized executives come in needing to look younger for job interviews. Executive placement firms actually recommend it.

As for what was bothering me, "The usual," I say. "I'm 50 and I'm falling apart. The main problem is that my belts keep getting bigger."

"You've tried diet and exercise?" he says, ethically.

"Yes," I answer, in all dishonesty.

He has me haul up my T-shirt and roll down my (best, of course) undershorts. He feels my gut. I half expect him to offer me a sonogram and say: "You have nothing to worry about, the baby's fine." The twins.

"You are a good candidate," he says, although for the money I think he'd say the same of Bob Dole.

"You have some excess tissue, but you're fairly thin overall and your skin still seems elastic." The last comment made me check to see if I'd removed my bicycle shorts. I also made a mental note that "Your skin is so elastic" might be a good pickup line to use later in life at retirement-home bars. (Note to my children: make sure the home has a full-service bar— don't sweat the crafts area.)

He allowed as how, in addition to sucking my gut, I could also use a brow-lift. Me? Low browed? He gave me a hand mirror to watch as he placed his thumb and forefinger on my eyebrows and lifted them. This gave me an alert look, but more than that: a surprised look.

The doctor said he could also get rid of those "worry lines" on my forehead (I'd always called them thinking lines), the bags beneath my eyes (each now the size of a clutch purse), and the crow's-feet (that now look more like triceratops tracks).

The facial overhaul would cost around, oh, seven grand. The gut would be about $1,800—that being the price of the first "area" suctioned—plus about another $900 for the "flanks," or love handles, plus around $1,500 for the operating room. When he said "flanks," I pictured one of those butcher-shop drawings with the dotted lines showing the various cuts of humans.

Total costs would be in the $11,000–$12,000 range, but, hell, you can't get a decent used car for that. Moreover, he was offering a special Face-Gut Combo price of nine to ten thousand—If You Act Now!

The whole facial thing scared me, especially the brow-lift. Can you imagine looking Absolutely Astonished!!! the rest of your life? "Could you just give me a sense of wonder?" I asked. He concluded that perhaps I wasn't such a great candidate after all, facially speaking.

The belly-buster operation did interest me, however, except he could promise only an inch or two loss around the waist— "*maybe* more." I was hoping for a foot! And the process sounded less than delightful. He explained that there would be bruising and swelling, and for the first week after surgery you wear rubber shorts (snug compression garments) with an elimination hole. Ish! My brother's Renault used to have an elimination hole. (The French really *are* disgusting, aren't they?) The second week you can remove the shorts but only for bathing. Total recovery can take up to six months. I asked if maybe he could just give me some snug compression garments now and forget the operation. "Does it work?" I asked. I mean I'd read some-where that Roseanne had liposuction, which is sort of like Mar-lon Brando doing an endorsement for Slimfast. "Will the fat come back?"

"No," he answered, but hedged a bit by saying there could possibly be some fat "migration" from other areas. And he said that if you go home and commence gluttonous eating you will gain weight, you just won't be as fat as you would have been. He said some people's fat cells have a greater "affinity" for fat than others. I think mine are pretty friendly.

I got dressed, mulling over my candidacy. You could get, like, a thousand pizzas for ten grand. At the elevator, a member of the custodial staff was vacuuming. I stared at the machine thinking maybe I should just wait for Hoover to come out with an attachment for home lipo use. The elevator doors opened. The passengers looked at me. I coughed.

Sex After 50
(This Will Be Brief)

*H*elp! My libido has fallen and I can't get up.

Gerontologists insist that diminished libido at this age is only in our heads, but with me, I swear it's the whole penis.

They assert that there is much scientific evidence to suggest that sexual desire and the capacity for sexual performance, enjoyment, and satisfaction does not dwindle in the least as one ages. (This is one place where President Clinton, 51, does actually lead by example.) In fact the experts claim sexual capacity increases—?!—and continues to exist well into the nineties. '92 was about it for me. August, as my wife recalls.

Despite what all these penile Pollyannas say, what we know is this: testicles begin shrinking at age 40; sperm production drops (as demand falters); and thickened prostate glands complicate ejaculation. Maximum ejaculatory distance declines in the aging man to five inches, from the younger man's average distance of roughly *two feet*—enough to impregnate a New Jersey Turnpike toll collector and never unbuckle your seat belt!

It's like Commies are dumping saltpeter into the nation's drinking water.

What's a man to do? It's a difficult, if not completely hard, question.

Women don't seem to lose libido like we do; but they never had it quite like we did—with our schwantzes calling all the shots. Now, I'm not sure who or what's calling the shots or from where.

I just know I don't give my fellow motorists the finger quite as much—and, naturally, things like this concern me. When I let a guy cut me off in traffic and I don't let fly the bird, do I still have the competitive, hormonal edge required for modern-day urban living?

I suffer the "middle-aged" malady of hypogonadism: loss of testosterone. They say this happens gradually, but I sort of felt it all at once, perhaps developing a serious leak the time my bicycle chain broke. Whether you lose it quickly or slowly, there are few sex offenders at the old-age home, and when one pops up they hold an awards banquet for the guy. I recall as a teenager working at a resort where an elderly desk clerk was roundly congratulated after informing everybody he'd experienced a hard-on the night before. I thought, "What a charming story," and quickly walked away before he segued into his bowel movements.

You know the old theory that if you took a jelly bean out of the jar every time you had sex before you were married, and put one back in every time you had sex after you were married, that you'd never get them all back in the jar? Lately I'd rather just *eat* the f——ing jelly beans.

Today, help is on the way for men who miss things like flipping off fellow motorists and reading *Playboy* one-handed.

It is: the miraculous transdermal testosterone patch. There are patches for everything these days. Patches for seasickness, patches for smokers, patches for dieters. (Does the diet patch go over the mouth?) Some people swear by patches and use them all. So, if you see a green-faced guy trying to throw up over the side of a cruise ship but he can't get close enough to the rail—he may have on the wrong patch. Same thing with a fat guy dragging his protruding pants zipper through the desserts at the smorgasbord: wrong patch.

Dr. Norm Mazer, of TheraTech, the company that developed the testosterone patch, argues: "We give eyeglasses to people to improve visual acuity, so why not testosterone?" Maybe because glasses don't make you hump the leg of the checkout lady at the grocery store?

In 1889, a 72-year-old French (of course!) scientist named Charles Brown-Sequard pioneered in the field by claiming he'd rejuvenated himself with liquid extract of guinea pig and dog testicles. Mmmm, blender drinks! I think we had that for lunch one day on ValuJet. Even if it works, where do you get fresh ingredients? The dumpster behind the vet's office?

It failed to catch on somehow, but a century later a test at Emory University showed that doses of testosterone resulted in lower cholesterol levels, improved sex drive, more muscle mass, and less loss of bone (which was the problem in the first place).

Now, it *may* also cause breast development, prostate growth, sterility, and increased risk of stroke—but what is all that when weighed against poontang?

Gotta date? You can place two Androderm testosterone patches anywhere on the body (although the face or crotch could prove counterproductive). They work for twenty-four hours. Isn't that, like, twenty-three hours and fifty minutes too long? Maybe they'll come out with a Testosterone-Lite patch.

All the other kinds of patches make you stop doing something. Testosterone patches are the only ones that make you *do* something. Or want to do it. At this age you have to find somebody to do it with. Which has always been the problem for guys. We spent hours as teenagers with our chemistry sets—making stink bombs, yes—but mainly trying to formulate Spanish Fly. We've spent thousands of dollars on jewelry, roses, candy, liquor, and your various eau de toilettes. Spent hours trying to talk women into doing it. Spent all of our energies and numerous brain cells trying to act sensitive and romantic. All toward the lofty, venerated goal of getting laid.

It has been a long, arduous, tortuous, expensive, exhausting, often humiliating, time-consuming quest—and now we're supposed to put on a testosterone patch to prolong it? No thanks. Could you hand me the remote? I want to see what's on ESPN and the Food Network.

There's all sorts of stuff at the health food store to restore romantic inclinations: turbo ginseng capsules, rhinoceros horn extract, powdered elk antlers—that kind of stuff. Central African yohimbé tree bark is currently in vogue. They do more than hug these trees.

A doctor I met in California (Dr. Neal Rouzier) convinced me to try taking capsules of DHEA (dehydroepiandrosterone), which males and females produce in their adrenal glands but which dwindles with age. DHEA helps fuel production of sex hormones, especially testosterone. They say it improves memory and libido, so I guess it could help a guy remember the names of those scores of women he'd be planking. Women taking excessive doses may develop facial hair, so it does make you more manly. Me? Nothing so far, although in the last week I have noticed myself watching the World Wrestling Federation a little more.

At this age, some men will begin experiencing "erectile dysfunction." As many as twenty million men are affected—not to mention their female companions. (Think banana futures.)

Once again, we are saved by the American Entrepreneur, who is already at work erecting (yes) a new chain of freestanding impotence centers. But will we have to park right in front of the damned things?

And Upjohn is running ads marketing the world's first commercial erection *injection*. Aieeee! Those ads are going to have to be good—really good.

You . . . inject . . . a fifth of a teaspoon of prescription medicine into the side of the penis. Or maybe you don't! If all men had to do this every time they had sex, we would each have a continent to ourselves right now.

"The number one disadvantage," admits one scientist, "is that you've got to put a needle in your penis." It's like saying there's a disadvantage to cleaning your ears with a .38 police special.

British physiologist G. S. Brindley demonstrated the product in a now famous 1983 address to the American Urological Association. At the end of his talk he announced that he had injected himself just before taking the podium (come to think of it, he did seem to be standing pretty far from the lectern). Then he lowered his pants and bared the dramatic proof. The product induces hourlong results, which means you have to get on with it before your coach turns into a pumpkin.

"It's all hydraulics," explains Irwin Goldstein, a doctor (not a romanticist) who counsels patients to just think of the injection as foreplay (and pistol-whipping as flirtatious?).

Sometimes the results don't go away for hours, and get this: the antidote is phenylephrine, which is Neo-Synephrine nose spray! So, gentlemen, if you have some Neo-Synephrine and an erection that just won't go away—don't forget to spray in that third nostril.

Speaking of which, there's a new system that pumps medicated pellets right into the ol' third nostril. What the hell? Why not just fill the damned thing with tree cement?

On less invasive fronts, some researchers are trying to develop an erection pill the user takes an hour before the act itself. A number of drugs are being tested, among them Pfizer's UK92480. It was tested as a heart-attack drug—and failed. But doctors visiting their patients noticed a curious side effect. Every patient looked as though a scout had pitched a pup tent under his bedcovers.

A few doctors are injecting fat into the penis, but those injections are said to sometimes cause "contour irregularities," which to me means they could make your unit look like something you'd find in a root cellar—a sweet potato, perhaps. Also, it seems injecting fat into penises could conceivably cause cholesterol problems in certain relationships.

Vacuum pumps are popular, both manual and electric. They draw blood into the penis: you slap a rubber band around the critter, and have at it. (Technically you could be dead! But, how to close the coffin?) Complaints are that the penis is sometimes cold and blue, but women in northern Minnesota have been working around that problem for years. One other drawback: if the pumper is too eager (which is virtually all the time) bruising may occur.

There are also—you may want to stand back a little, folks—spring-loaded implants. Another implant is an inflatable reservoir in the penis attached to a squeeze pump in the scrotum. It's like the old Barbie doll: crank Barbie's arm and her breasts grow. Now, it's: squeeze Ken's balls . . .

One thing is clear. Although our reproductive mission is complete, this generation that invented free love is not about to just shelve it. Where will it all end? With patches, pumps, and pills—and black-lace Depends, perhaps.

Over 50
Sex Tips

By All Means Continue to Enjoy Sex after 50, but Please . . .

1. Only with a Registered Nurse.
2. Or at Least a Trained Professional. (Men, try the "Escort" and "Masseuse" sections of your Yellow Pages. Women, try proffering a $100 tip to the cute guy with the tool belt who's doing your tongue-and-groove flooring or Roto-Rootering your pipes.)
3. Try to keep It Outside Your Own Immediate Demographic Group—target the prime 18–49 audience.
4. Or, Just Keep It to Yourself. At this point why drag others into this ugly business?

Warning

If You Choose to Continue Having Sex with Your Same-Age Spouse, Remember . . .

1. Never Look Down (from the Missionary Position). It's like mountain climbing. What you see down below can be very scary and can cause a fall.

2. Keep Your Shirt On. I don't mean slow down and take it easy. I mean really: Keep Your Shirt On! And your pants, your shoes—whatever it takes to keep you looking your best.

3. Remove Your Glasses. Particularly during oral sex. Moreover, removing eyewear blurs your vision, acting like gauze on the lens during Elizabeth Taylor close-ups.

4. Go with "Mood" Lighting. Remove all light bulbs, and tape wall switches firmly in their "off" positions.

5. Enjoy a Glass of Wine. A bottle is better. 190-proof Everclear is best.

6. Keep It Under Wraps. Pull up the covers, as a courtesy.

7. Think of Others. (On *Baywatch*.)

8. Plan Ahead. If you know, for example, that you just may be having sex next Valentines Day, schedule liposuction for October to give wounds a chance to heal and swelling to go down.

9. Practice Safe Sex. Not condoms, idiot! Have oxygen tanks and nitroglycerin pills bedside, along with a blood-pressure monitor to avoid dreaded Nelson Rockefeller syndrome.

10. Keep It Simple. With your memory, you don't want to be continually stopping to refer to note cards—a turnoff.

Don'ts

1. Avoid So-called Romantic Getaway Weekends at "Special" Motels. Too much time together, too many mirrors.

2. Avoid Role-playing. At this age most of the roles are on *Murder, She Wrote*.

3. And Avoid So-called Marital Aids. There is a terrible story of the aging, farsighted woman fumbling around in the dark

on her nightstand, looking for her cordless vibrator but instead picking up a small clock radio and . . . well the only saving grace was that the alarm happened to be set for that very moment, and when it went off . . .

Rolling Stones
& Fossils

*D*ATELINE, ROLLING STONES NORTH AMERI-
CAN TOUR, NEW YORK—Two nubile nym-
phets clad in torn jeans and little else slink
across our path. My brother-in-law, Herb, shoots them a flirtatious smile. I laugh, inappropriately.

But, c'mon. I mean, *what if* by some impossible luck we
had actually *picked up* these girls? I could just see them standing there in the parking lot while Herb and I frantically fumbled
to remove the baby seat so we could all fit into his Taurus station wagon. And would they actually believe that "This is
mom's car"?

We have momentarily forgotten how old we are. But! So
has the band. One member, for example, was well into his 50s,
and married to a 19-year-old whose mother was dating his son.
If they hit it off, his son could become his father-in-law. (Jag-
ger's a grandfather, and looks it.)

This is a time for reunion tours, a time for slathering on the
Oil of Olay, buying a new pair of "Relaxed Fit" jeans, piling
into the Aerostar, and heading over to the local stadium to hear
Dylan, the Who, Kinks, Jefferson Airplane, the Bee Gees,
Doobie Brothers, Allman Brothers, and America (who still sing

"been through the desert on a horse with no name" and I still don't get it).

I'll bet when the Bee Gees sing "Stayin' Alive" these days it takes on a special poignancy with aging audiences. And isn't it time that Jerry and the Pacemakers made a comeback?

The Stones tickets were $100 apiece—the price of a good Weedeater!—but that's not much more than a bad Broadway play. Moreover, actuarial tables suggest that this could be the last time the Stones and I can get together—live. (Actually, it appeared that two Stones might have already passed on and were appearing thanks to modern advances in taxidermy procedures.)

Besides, looking around during the concert, I realize I'd pay *anything* to see groups of heterosexual males in their Giants and Jets jackets fast dancing with each other to "Satisfaction." To their credit, they did sit out the slow numbers.

They don't dance *well*, mind you. Middle-class suburban types are still essentially a-rhythmic, same as they were at Woodstock, and now they all seem a step slower as well. Reunion concerts are beginning to take on the look of aerobics classes at a Century Village retirement community.

The guy to our right starts complaining about lower back pain sustained from standing on his chair for two and a half hours. There is a whole new set of concert concerns. The people in the EMS tent are standing around, prepared to bring people down from bad acid trips, but tending instead to a man concerned that his blood pressure has gone too high.

Acid? They weren't even selling *beer* on the field where we were sitting, and security forces were patting people down as they came in, confiscating alcohol.

Luckily, they got our bottles of Old Crow and Captain Morgan's Spiced Rum. Allow me to explain: we ran into a liquor store on the way where a gentleman was passed out on the floor with a smile on his face. "We're in a hurry," Herb said to the clerk, "just give us what he's having."

Minutes before, I'd rushed into the men's room at work with a duffel bag of denim in an attempt to transform myself from work-a-daddy geek to moderately hip concertgoer.

"Don't I have *anything* black?" I'd cried the night before, tearing through my closet. My wife, still smarting over not being invited to the concert, suggested: "How about that charred barbecue apron."

I used to have cool clothes, now my closet was filled with all of this dull . . . *Kremlin*-wear. Would a blue blazer be sporty enough?

I did have this one old pair of black jeans . . . if . . . I . . . could . . . just . . . get . . . the . . . damned . . . things . . . buttoned!

I tried buttoning my top shirt button, for a touch of attitude, but this only made me look like a dweeb—Bill Gates on weekends. Wasn't much I could do to be cool at this point. It was like trying to learn the entire Spanish language the night before the final exam.

Herb was waiting in my office, wearing an earring, a black leather jacket with a white scarf through one of the epaulets, and silver-toed black boots. Next to him, I looked like I was going out to mow the lawn.

In the Taurus wagon, he strapped a spiked dog collar on his wrist, put a Stones tape on full blast, and drove recklessly—really the only way *to* drive to a Stones concert, I suppose. I wanted to put on my seat belt, but found that the shoulder harness inhibited drinking the Captain Morgan's—an absolute necessity for passengers in a vehicle careening nearly out of control through New York traffic.

At a stoplight, a man offering to clean our windshield with a Crisco-impregnated rag approached the car. He was having a bad day, and smelled of . . . Captain Morgan's? Herb passed him the bottle, he took a pull and gave it back. "Gee," I thought to myself, "I sure wish he'd used a straw."

Three hours before the Stones went on, everyone had already arrived at Shea Stadium, where tailgating-with-a-twist was under way. Some fans looked as though they were still here from the Stones' last swing through town three weeks before. Hey, listen, man, once you've got a good parking spot . . .

There were a lot more wing tips and fewer bare feet than I recalled seeing at these things. Gone were the groups of guys sitting in a circle smoking hash. One guy was high on some painkillers he had left over from his ligament operation the year before, but there was far less staggering around here than you see in the parking lot before a National Football League match-up. You know, the Long Island carpeting magnate who stumbles over his barbecue grill and impales himself on the hood ornament of his Town Car?

Inside, lots of middle-aged people were standing around with yellow plastic shopping bags full of $20 T-shirts. "Gotta take something home to the kids!" yelled one hawker who knew his target audience well.

The day had been extraordinarily warm, a last gasp, but now it was getting a bit nippy. The word "cryogenics" popped into my mind. The scent of anti-aging gel hung heavy in the air. A cigarette of uneven proportions was passed down the row.

"What time are the Stones coming on, anyway?" a woman asked me, as the second warm-up band finished playing. "We've got a sitter."

"I can dig it," I replied, and passed the cigarette down the line.

Turning Republican

The older you get the more conservative you become. I damned near voted Republican in the last presidential election (thinking that Dole, like Gotti, is a better *person* than Clinton)—but was out of town.

Warning Signs That You May Be Turning Republican

1. Test-Drive Cadillac.
2. Think affirmative action should be restricted to boxing and lawn-care professions.
3. Find Sonny Bono's remarks thought provoking.
4. Support "use 'em or lose 'em" stance on handicapped parking spaces.
5. Object to "La Cucaracha" replacing "Silent Night" in school Christmas pageant.
6. Suddenly stop buying "Newman's Own" salad dressing.
7. Think two-man luge is homo honeymoon.
8. Can no longer seem to fast dance properly.
9. Think The Freemen had a point.

10. Have a taste for tangy buffalo spotted owl wings.
11. Linger on Limbaugh when flipping through stations.
12. Consider golfers "athletes" and golf courses to be all the protected lands a country really needs.
13. Always remark on Hillary's calves.
14. Think Dan Quayle is smarter than some people think.
15. Consider Kwanzaa bullshit.
16. Think Brooks Brothers may be going "a bit mod."
17. Oppose changing your traditional old college mascot from "the drunken, scalping redskins" to something slightly more politically correct.
18. Favor replacing current welfare system with inner-city "Up with People" concert tour.
19. Believe Second Amendment covers private ownership of certain surface-to-air missiles for duck-hunting sportsmen.
20. Think seeing John Tesh on PBS is a positive sign.

The Birthday

*P*eople ask me: "Bill, what's the *best* way to celebrate your fiftieth birthday?"

Well, heck, no two people are alike, but as for me, well, I always suggest: "Whip yourself up a nice birthday cake, turn on the oven and stick your head in it."

The National Opinion Research Center says half of all those 50 years of age have gone through some traumatic event in the past year, the highest percentage of any age bracket. No shit! Their birthdays!

Some people go a bit mad when they turn 50 and do bizarre things on their birthdays.

Designer Josie Natori practiced Schuman and Rachmaninoff on the piano every day for three years and gave a fiftieth birthday concert at Carnegie Hall, where Tchaikovsky, Toscanani, and Horowitz had played before her. Since she was understandably a mite nervous, her performance was not perfect, but she hadn't invited any music critics to her birthday party. She had flown in friends and relatives from around the world, rented the entire St. Luke's Orchestra as a backup band,

and rented the Hall itself—for a grand birthday party price of half a million dollars.

Natalie Moore did a flying trapeze act on her fifthtieth. And has pictures to prove it. A large one framed in her kitchen shows Natalie completely extended with arms outstretched, flying about thirty feet in the air toward a man who's hanging upside down by his legs on a swing with his arms out toward hers.

Her friends were not completely surprised. Natalie is a Citicorp bank vice president in investment services, which makes her *sound* staid enough, but she had previously demonstrated a bent toward aberrant behavior. She'd mortified friends and family by quitting her twenty-year career at the bank at one point to scuba dive in New Zealand, sell china at Saks in New York, and take courses in holistic auto maintenance and shamanism, "where we beat drums and pretended to be raccoons."

Some months before the big birthday she vacationed in Eleuthera, where she had first tried the trapeze ten years before on a setup for some circus performers. The pros agreed to teach her some basic moves.

Understand, now, that in order to even get *to* the trapeze swing you first have to climb a twenty-five-foot ladder and walk across a narrow board. This leaves me out.

"Then all you have to do," she explains, "is get on the bar, swing out, get the bar locked behind your knees, fly off at the right time, and grab the catcher. On the return, you let go of his arms, flip in the air, and catch the swing. And to get down you do a flip in the air and land in the net. That's it." Ohhh! And I thought it might be something *difficult*.

It was. She learned a more advanced move: the bird's nest. "In this one," she explains, "all you do is hang by your ankles, then reach back and grab the bar behind you, forming a cradle, or bird's nest." Ohhh, that's all you do.

The pro acrobats decided to put on a little show for the vacationers, using a couple of the amateurs. The guy who went before Natalie crashed into the catcher, which was not a real confidence booster. But she, in her turquoise Lycra tights, performed the bird's nest, perfectly.

For her fiftieth birthday, she traveled to Port St. Lucie, Florida, where there was a flying-trapeze setup.

As a warm-up that day, she took (and completed) a step-aerobics class with a lot of women half her age, she went slalom water skiing and Rollerblading.

Then she went to the trapeze. She performed her repertoire and added a big one for the Big Five-Oh: the flying splits. This one sort of defies description (plus the laws of physics), but a photograph shows Natalie swinging out in the splits position with only one of her thighs touching the bar.

"There was no audience," she said. "I did it for myself" and went home.

It happens in America about eleven thousand times a day now—someone turning 50—far outstripping the casualty rate for hunting accidents and car wrecks combined. Everywhere you look, someone's turning 50: Candice Bergen, Donald Trump, Susan Sarandon. O. J. Simpson turns 50 in 1997. I'd so hoped he wouldn't.

Four of our friends here in town turned 50 just this month. They have had mixed results with their fiftieth-birthday parties. For Ward's fiftieth, his wife, Susie, purchased about forty tickets to see the Four Tops and we gave him a surprise greeting at the theater. What fun! I mean, who could forget "My Girl"?

(No, that was the Temptations.) "Tracks of My Tears"? (No, Smokey Robinson.) It had been almost three decades, so we were having a little trouble figuring out what we were going to be hearing.

"I Can't Help Myself"! Now there was one, but unfortunately the Four Tops never got to it because twenty minutes into their performance the lead singer, Levi, started complaining about the heat, said he didn't feel well, and quit. The remaining three Tops announced that the remainder of the show was canceled. Such are the perils of parties where the guests are pretending to be young again, but the entertainers have a tougher job pulling it off. *Of course* the entertainers don't feel well! They should be in the talent show at the home once a year, not out on tour! The only saving grace was that we all repaired to a local bar where Ward was thoroughly humiliated by receiving a three-foot-tall blowup of a highly unflattering photograph of himself in a swimming suit, and various and sundry bad acrylic wigs for his balding pate. As for the Four Tops, they rescheduled the performance for some weeks later, but, alas, canceled again. They hadn't gotten any younger.

Unlike most natural catastrophes, turning 50 doesn't just happen to you one day.

It haunts you. You think about it, reflect upon it, worry about it, are in a bad mood about it and spend a lot of time vowing not to be—for days, weeks, months, and years ahead of the natural disaster itself.

I didn't have a fiftieth-birthday party. Didn't want one. I was totally bummed and gave Jody strict instructions not to buy me anything, not to mention it to anyone, and especially not to have a party. Nothing. She honored my request, which was the best present of all. Denial works for me.

She's thrown great surprise birthday parties for me in the (distant) past, once in my late 20s and once in my late 30s—complete with obligatory obscene gifts (such as the foot-long dildo that my brother-in-law's girlfriend secretly took home) and impromptu party games like tumbling in the living room and cake throwing in the dining area.

But now, I simply couldn't endure a bunch of insulting cards about my bowel movements, and those dreadful gifts—boxes of Depends, and throw pillows inscribed "Oh How Nifty, Bill Is Fifty." Or worse yet, a lap-dancing stripper. It just isn't the same, somehow, with your kids watching. I didn't even want a cake. For your fiftieth they make them in the shape of a tombstone. And the candles! You have to buy *five* boxes (of twelve) to get enough, and stick some on the side of the cake because there isn't room on top, and ask your kids to help you blow them all out, and take the batteries out of the smoke alarm. Unh-unh.

Jody thought my attitude weird (she says the fortieth is worse for women), until she came to within a few days of her own fiftieth and proclaimed that she, too, would be horrified by a big party. So we kept it small, one hundred guests on the porch for a front-yard fireworks display on the order of New York City's and with several visits by armed police officers. But we called it a Fourth of July party with no mention of any birthday—except for the big cake with lots of candles on top, and the singing of "Happy Fourth of July to You."

Michael Lamar papered his Atlanta subdivision with signs that read "Ain't It Nifty Sandy's 50" (Sandy being his wife), along with balloons and arrows on the pavement leading to her driveway. Cute, sufficient grounds for murder, and no jury of her true peers (women over 50) would convict her.

Bill Shrieves of Virginia did fifty consecutive sky dives. A friend of my computer fixer rented a Dodge Viper (top speed 160 mph) and drove really fast for a week. Looking for something a little more spiritual, Pam Blankenheim camped alone on a cliff overlooking the Snake River in south central Idaho, reflecting on her condition—the *last* thing I would want to do. Let's hope she didn't actually *look* at her reflection in those waters.

Paul Fingerote's wife had a plane fly over with a sign reading "HAPPY HALF CENTURY, PAUL" as he watched a baseball game at San Francisco's Candlestick Park in a luxury box with a butler.

Some regress, holding slumber parties and sweet-sixteen parties they never had. Another woman, who had been downsized out of a job at IBM and then underwent gallbladder surgery, held a prom with the theme of "A Hedonist's Delight." She hoped everyone would wind up naked in a hot tub—not a pretty sight at 50.

Some go on trips they never took—or maybe that last trip to Europe without the walker. Grim stuff. I went to France for the first time at 50, not because I was 50 but because my son was in school there for a semester and I wanted to make sure he was all right. Didn't actually see much of the boy.

Allegra Bennett of Baltimore created a calendar for 1997 with photographs of women 50 and older—one you won't see hanging in too many auto-repair shops or army barracks.

Vivian Duffield had a half-million-dollar fiftieth-birthday party for herself in England's Eltham Palace with dancing bears, "wenches" (!), and the King and Queen of Greece (what do *they* rent for?).

*　　*　　*

Nothing is too good for ourselves. The trend among boomers, not surprisingly, are Celebrations of Myself. Of myself, by myself, for myself. Boomers take out party loans, for chrissake.

Caryl McCalla of New York planned a full year of parties to celebrate her fiftieth birthday, including (but not limited to): a disco party at a New York club; a pajama party at the Waldorf Astoria; a Belmont racetrack outing; a dinner cruise around Manhattan for one hundred; a formal birthday dance at the Plaza Hotel; a weekend in the Bahamas; and a trip to Europe.

Lavish, yes, but it was the least she could do, for someone like herself.

Boomers turning 50 don't wait around for friends to throw them birthday parties. Too risky. You might find out you don't have one (one party, one friend).

While some boomers are taking out party loans, the Sultan of Brunei just held a pretty nice fiftieth celebration without one. It was hardly necessary for a party that cost an estimated $25 million to fly in two thousand guests to have their cake and listen to Michael Jackson, too. Consternation was expressed by invitees like the Prince of Wales, who was uncertain what to give a man with one hundred Rolls-Royces, his own Boeing 747, and $33 billion. (How about Bermuda?)

"I have a tough time with the whole idea of presents," Donald Trump told me on a recent birthday. It was June and he confided he still hadn't opened a lot of his Christmas presents yet.

The Donald just turned 50, celebrating as tastefully as he knew how, with four hundred people invited in to dine on Swedish meatballs (the official meatball of the Professional Bowlers Association), to admire an ice sculpture of then wife

Marla as a mermaid, and to rub shoulders with Indianapolis 500 Parade–caliber celebrities like Morgan Fairchild.

As the nation's Boomer-in-Chief, Bill Clinton set the standard for extravagance, holding his fiftieth-birthday party at Radio City (not the party room at McDonalds, as many would have guessed).

I could hide out when I turned 50 and few knew, but when you're the President the whole world knows—especially when you hold your party at Radio City. When Clinton turned 50, the usually staid CIA joined in the fun in its daily briefing, reporting that Moscow had declared a national security alert after detecting an unidentified heat source in New York City, but then discovered the blaze was coming from the 50 candles atop the President's birthday cake.

It was a typical yuppie party—a lucrative affair. Clinton probably outdid every kid who ever had a birthday party for himself by raking in not scads of Nintendo games or Barbies but *$10 million in cash gifts* (for his campaign)! Sure beats that crap from Toys "R" Us.

Based on this I would tell American kids: you've got to set minimums, like Vegas, for getting in the game. Like, a Super Mario Brothers or better or you don't get into the birthday party. Clinton set a $250 minimum, but if you wanted to stick around for food and a piece of cake it was another $10,000!   .

And listen to this: he pulled in another *fifteen thousand guests* by simulcasting the party to groups at other locations where each guest had to cough up the $100 minimum. This is an unprecedented take in the annals of birthday-party history.

Smart kid, Clinton. He must have been an *unbelievable*

trick-or-treater! With lists of donors, what they gave last year, and trick-or-treat phone banks: "Hello I'm calling on behalf of Billy Clinton, who unfortunately can't personally make it to each and every house in Arkansas this year. We noticed you gave out small, bite-sized Snickers last year and wondered if we could put you down for a full-sized bar this year? And could you Fedex it?"

Yes, Clinton did have a professional birthday-party planner, the guy who produced the Academy Awards show and the Miss America Pageant. Whoopi Goldberg was the emcee and guest performers and celebrities included Jon Bon Jovi, Aretha Franklin, Carly Simon, Smokey Robinson, Kenny Rogers, Stevie Wonder, Tim Conway, Olympians Carl Lewis and Keri Strug, Ted Danson, and (one stroke of brilliance) a videotaped appearance rather than a personal appearance by Roger Clinton. Leslie Nielson and Maya Angelou were also there—probably their first appearance on the same card.

Sister Mary Kee, his second-grade teacher, came onstage to say she had to give him a "C" in comportment (and that was *before* Paula Jones, Jennifer Flowers et al.), and said she'd talked with his mother about his excessive eagerness to speak (*before* he began making filibusterous convention addresses).

Tony Bennett sang the upbeat "The Best Is Yet to Come" to an admiring, but disbelieving, audience.

The Clinton affair, if you'll excuse the overused expression, was patterned after a forty-fifth-birthday gala staged at Madison Square Garden for President Kennedy—the one where Marilyn Monroe sang a breathy "Happy Birthday, Mr. President." It was learned some years later that she had also given a gift.

News accounts reported that all of this left President Clinton "thick voiced and teary" and doing that lip-biting thing, but then so did the end of the Arch Deluxe introductory special at McDonalds.

In time it can get better, I'm told. You turn 51, and you don't have to start worrying about 60 for several more years.

First
Boomer

I was so shocked when I got my AARP card in the mail," James Sickler said, "that I threw it in the garbage."

That's typical. James Otis Sickler Jr. is the first of 76 million baby boomers to be born between 1946 and 1964, and the first Boomer to turn 50.

Seventy-six million! That famed Alfred Eisenstaedt photograph of a sailor kissing a girl in Times Square on V-J Day didn't begin to tell the story of the monumental, historic, unprecedented wave of . . . fecundity . . . about to hit U.S. shores with the return of 14 million heroic, victorious, horny troops. Long war.

Fecundity. You know, screwing! 76 million! My God, there must have been nights in Levittown (buy a house for $58 down!) when the whole town was shaking. Get me the local Richter scale readings for those dates.

Starting January 1, 1996, about 11,000 baby boomers a day began celebrating their fiftieth birthdays, first James Sickler, then one every seven-and-a-half seconds. This will continue unabated for ten years before tapering off slightly. This, while the government stands idly by and does nothing to alleviate the pain of this massive national catastrophe.

One turning fifty every seven-and-a-half seconds means, of course, that something else—infinitely more fun!—was happening every seven and a half seconds back in 1945, correct?

My neighborhood was crawling with kids, always more than enough for a pickup baseball game. There was a neighborhood near my house where returning servicemen and their families were housed while they attended college on the G.I. Bill. It was nicknamed "Sperm Village." Had to be careful riding your bike through there, wheels would go right out from under you.

Records show James Sickler was born one half second after midnight, January 1, 1946—although how they know that I don't know. I guess the delivery-room nurses over at Missouri Baptist had stop watches.

"I understand there are twins in California born right after me at one second after midnight," Sickler said. No glory in being the second and third baby boomers born. And, anyway, that was Pacific time. You know, there must have been some babies born earlier than Sickler on eastern time. I guess someone decided that the baby boom would officially begin on central standard time.

As First Boomer, he has gained a measure of fame, having appeared on TV and in newspapers. His baby picture appeared on the front page of the *National Enquirer*—probably the first baby picture without two heads to appear in that publication in some time.

Fame *and* fortune? "Nah," he said. No endorsement contracts. "A radio guy in Florida was supposed to send me some T-shirts, but he never did." He said that he is known locally for playing the role of Simon the Zealot every year in the community Passion play, however.

James thinks he was a fairly typical boomer kid, although he thinks that the notion of all baby boomers being somehow alike—when some of them are fully 18 years apart—is a bit hokey.

In high school, he drove his '64 Mercury Cyclone around too fast; his favorite album was the Beatles' *Sgt. Pepper's* (still has his copy of *The White Album*); he did not protest the Vietnam War, but he didn't go either; never had long hair and never smoked dope. Jaaaames? "Really," he said, "I never did."

He thinks he's still fairly typical. He is a machinist at McDonnell-Douglas. His hair is graying and he's fighting a weight problem, having gained twenty pounds in the last two years. Well, not exactly *fighting* the weight problem, just kind of monitoring it. He does "not really" exercise and he does "not really" eat health food. Pizza-with-everything-but-anchovies is his favorite food.

"My wife doesn't really give me a hard time about eating pizza," he said, "just about eating the *whole* pizza."

His doctor made him stop drinking beer, which does not exactly thrill him.

He lives in a ranch home in New Melle, Missouri, forty miles from St. Louis, with his second wife, Shirlee, two of his five stepchildren, and four dogs. He drives a family minivan, but likes to tinker with his "grabber blue" '71 Mustang. "It's not as easy getting up from under it as it used to be," he noted.

The former hundred-yard dash man in high school now chases his grandchildren around. He has six.

Asked what was the best part about turning 50, there was a long silence before he finally said: "Do you think my car insurance will go down?" I told him that to my knowledge car insurance doesn't do that.

He said he wasn't really too bummed over his fiftieth birthday, but his wife was—perhaps realizing that her turn was coming. He said his friends gave him "funny" gifts like an "Over the Hill" hat and a cane with a rearview mirror.

"They couldn't treat me too badly, though," he said, "because they're all right behind me." They and 76 million others.

How to Recognize the Onset of Menopause

- You sell your home heating system at a yard sale (Hot flashes)
- The person you sleep with complains about snow piling up on the bed (Nightsweats)
- Your husband jokes that instead of buying a woodstove, he's using you to heat the family room this winter. Rather than just saying you are not amused, you shoot him (Mood swings)
- Your write Post-it notes with your kids' names on them (Memory loss)
- Your husband chirps, "Hi honey, I'm home," and you reply, "Well if it isn't Ozzie F——ing Nelson" (Irritability)
- You change underwear after every sneeze (Mild incontinence)
- The phenobarbitol dose that wiped out the Heaven's Gate cult gives you 4 hours of decent rest (Sleeplessness)
- You find guacamole in your hair after a Mexican dinner (Fatigue)
- You need Jaws Of Life to help you out of car after returning home from Italian restaurant (Sudden weight gain)

- You think Antonio Banderas is "OK, I guess" (Libido loss)
- You ask Jiffy Lube to put you up on a hoist (Dryness)
- You take a sudden interest in "Wrestlemania" (Female hormone deficiency)
- You're on so much estrogen you take your Brownie troop on a field trip to Chippendales (Hormone therapy)

Red-Hot
Mamas

*H*orse urine. And horse urine
futures. That's my investment tip for today.

Premarin is an estrogen product made for humans from the
urine of pregnant horses. It's reportedly one of the biggest-
selling drugs in America right now, as baby boomers hit menopause and fight nature with estrogen-replacement programs
designed to relieve hot flashes, sleep disturbances, memory loss,
irritability, and other ravages of time.

There is more horse urine in the jam-packed meeting room
in New Britain, Connecticut, this evening than in the paddock
area at Churchill Downs.

In the film *Fried Green Tomatoes*, Jessica Tandy tells Kathy
Bates to "get yourself some hormones," after bouts of hot
flashes and irritability—and most of the women here tonight
have done just that, with progesterone chasers.

"It's helped," says one, "except that I think it's making me
fatter, which makes me irritable and depressed all over again."

"You know the expression 'T & A'?" asks another estrogen
user. "Well my T's are getting bigger and so is my A."

*   *   *

This is a meeting of a group called the Red-Hot Mamas, and if they could harness the heat that these 400 menopausal women are flashing off, they could probably shut down the New Britain power plant.

"I'm having a hot flash right now," announces a woman with a face the color of her scarlet sweater.

"Four Hundred Menopausal Women!" Forget *Twister* and *Volcano*, this has the makings of a real Hollywood disaster thriller. But they weren't snarling as much as I'd feared as they congregated to talk and learn about the myriad perils—and mere pains in the butt—of menopause.

If menopause was "the silent passage," it certainly isn't anymore.

"I used to wonder," says Phyllis, "what my mother was doing at home in her slip with the windows open. I thought she'd flipped."

Now, we have monthly meetings of the Red-Hot Mamas, where topics range from hormone therapies to homeopathic treatments and home remedies. "Don't even think about drinking red wine," advises one hot flash sufferer. "Or eating tacos!"

Karen Giblin started the group (now officially called Prime Plus/Red-Hot Mamas) five years ago in Ridgefield, Connecticut, and it has grown to 30 sites in ten states. (There are now 13 million women in the 45–54 age group and there will be 19 million by the year 2000, she notes.)

"I have all the symptoms myself," Karen says. "I had hot flashes that were like rubbing Ben-Gay all over my body.

"Right now it's weight gain. I went to buy a swimming suit, looked in the mirror and my body looked like a shar-pei. They told me to buy tall women's suits to hide more, but I'm 5' 4".

"I have Post-it notes all over the place because I can't remember anything. I'm in the springtime of my senility.

"I have night sweats so bad I sleep with the windows open. My dog, Lacey, a Westie, whines and burrows under the covers."

The women describe their hot flashes as "a lot like the electric chair" and "like I just ate a jar of chili peppers." One woman tells of turning off the heat and opening windows when her husband leaves the house, then cranking up the thermostat to 90 degrees right before he returns home.

The guest speaker is Suzie Humphries, a sprightly, redheaded Texan, who is in the midst of telling me of her past menopausal battles, when suddenly she loses her train of thought and asks of no one in particular: "What's my point?" She isn't being funny, just forgetful—as we, the aging, are wont to be. "I write myself a lot of notes," she says. They read 'Eat' and 'Bathe.' "

She describes her husband's mid-life crisis. "He walked in one day and said, 'Let's leave Dallas' "—their longtime home, where they both had successful careers going. They moved to a tiny Texas town where he built his own airstrip.

Some in the audience say menopause has them a little depressed and Suzie has advice: "Give in to it! Totally. Resisting it causes stress and pain. Don't go to the psychiatrist! He'll tell you to go be with *people*. No people want to be with you when you're depressed! Stay home. Put on your old robe, the terry cloth one with the wine stain. Do not wash your hair. Look at yourself in the mirror with the mascara running down from your crying. You'll look so ugly it will make you more depressed. Go to bed, pull the covers over your head and really cry. Think of sad things. Really get the tears rolling. Think of someone who dumped you. Think of how your daddy always loved your brother more. Let the tears flow from the top of your head to your toes. Cry and sob for two hours and I guarantee you you'll eventually say, 'God I'm sick of this!' then get up and go have some Mexican food!"

Men don't attend these meetings. "One did once," says Karen Giblin, "and he said he was there to meet women."

Is there male menopause? It's an open question in the medical community, where studies show that men do experience significant hormonal changes and do run off with personal trainers half their age—sometimes on Harleys.

This would be your Mid-life Crisis, and can backfire. When a man tries to act like he did when he was young and he can't, it only makes him feel worse. (When running off, always pack a bottle of ginseng and a box of Androderm testosterone patches in the glove compartment).

The male version of menopause is called andropause or viropause. Sex hormone levels drop (but not as fast as women's do) and some men experience hot flashes, night sweats, fatigue, depression, and losses of energy and libido—just like women. Some men seek testosterone-replacement therapy in the form of tablets, capsules, gels, patches, and slow-release implants. Watch the dosage. If you get up in the morning with the urge to invade Poland, it's probably high.

Potency ebbs. We question our vitality. We question our values:

Sample Ethical Question for Menopausal Men:

Gauguin, a Parisian stockbroker, left his family at 43 and went to Tahiti to paint bare-breasted native women.

That was bad . . . right? Guys always get that one wrong.

Elderly
Children

hen you're fifty you have to lie not only about your own age, but also about the ages of your children. Otherwise things won't add up. There's always some math nut in the crowd who'll question your veracity:

QUESTION: "HMMM. YOU SAY YOU'RE THIRTY-TWO, BUT YOUR SON IS IN COLLEGE?"

SUGGESTED ANSWER: "YES. WE'RE OF APPALACHIAN DESCENT. THE KIDS ARE ACTUALLY PRODUCTS OF MY THIRD MARRIAGE, HELD DURING THE JUNIOR-SENIOR PROM, SINCE WE WERE ALL DRESSED UP ANYWAY."

OPTIONAL ANSWER: "WHY, YES. HE'S IN HIS THIRD YEAR OF MEDICAL SCHOOL, ACTUALLY. PERHAPS YOU SAW HIM ON THE COVER OF *MENSA* MAGAZINE. OR DON'T YOU SUBSCRIBE?"

At the office fax:
Jack looks tired and disheveled. "God," he whines, "my

one-year-old was up coughing half the night. She woke up our three-year-old, and we couldn't get him up for nursery school."

"Yeah," gripes Jill, "my twenty-month-old has been sick all winter. The older one brings home every disease known to medical science from kindergarten."

I stand silently, waiting to fax, hoping not to be brought into this infantile conversation. But Jack turns and asks: "You have kids, don't you, Bill?"

"Yes," I answer, curtly.

"How're they doing?" Jill wants to know.

"Fine, fine," I answer. And they are fine: no arrests, no convictions, no pregnancies, no drug rehab.

Then Jill asks the dreaded follow-up: "How old are your little ones now?"

Little ones!? Let's see, does she mean the 6'4" boy or the 5'10" girl? I don't answer right away. "Middle-aged," is what I'm thinking; "positively elderly" by comparison.

"Well, let's see," I say, fumbling for some sort of positive spin I can put on this, "believe it or not, I have a daughter who's . . . a . . . teenager already."

What I do not say is that she's *been* a teenager for four years and is closer to not being a teenager than she is to becoming one. I certainly do not say that my son is *no longer* a teenager.

And the hell of it is: Jack and Jill do not express shock. C'mon. I mean show a little astonishment. Be polite, gasp a little, put your hand to your chest, stagger backwards and exclaim: "No! You *can't* have a child *that* old!"

"Amazing," says Jack, as if he were standing before the Prehistoric Man exhibit at the Museum of Natural History.

Jill presses the inquisition: "What grade is she in?" Jesus, Jill, did you used to work for the DA's office or something?

I'm afraid to lie at this point. Jill is coming on like Marcia Clark and she might produce birth certificates or DNA evidence.

"Sophomore," I say. "Smart kid," I add, hoping they'll think maybe she skipped a grade or two. (Actually she's a junior. I had to lie a *little* bit.)

"And," queries Jack, sort of the Christopher Darden of the prosecutorial team, "don't you have a son, too?"

"That's right, two," I reply. Two years and 216 months.

At fifty, most of us have . . . elderly . . . children.

You have no idea who the hell this Tickle Me Elmo character is, and you don't really care—unless your *grand*child desperately wants one. (And that is the only way one wants a Tickle Me Elmo—desperately or not at all.) My high school girlfriend has been a grandmother for, like, ten years! And we have a good friend who bounces her grandchild on her knee while talking to my wife about her boyfriends.

At this age you *could* conceivably want a Tickle Me Elmo for your own toddler if you happen to be one of those aging "Start Over Dads" who've jettisoned their first (at a minimum) wives, started new families, and are celebrated by Gail Sheehy as now having the time to be "fully nurturant." (Has anyone seen that box of nausea patches?)

Tony Randall just fathered a child at age seventy-seven (although he may not realize it), Clint Eastwood is having a baby at sixty-five, and George Plimpton at sixty-nine has little twins. More power to them and may there always be wheelchair ramps at the PTA meetings.

The thing I don't like about Start Over Dads is that they're always fighting with the baby over the disposable diapers.

*   *   *

My kids are grown, and lately I find myself starting to think I'd really rather see "No Children" sections in restaurants than "No Smoking" ones. I'm starting to become a bit less tolerant of the wee bastards. Secondary smoke is nothing compared to secondary diapers, secondary tantrums, and secondary parenting: "Zachary Jedidiah, if you throw any more spaghetti on that man I'm going to have to consider threatening you with no sprinkles on your ice-cream sundae, and this time I think I mean it."

I find a lot of today's new parents annoying. Giving their children "time-outs" for slaying their friends; strapping safety helmets on them every time they walk down a flight of stairs; displaying those stupid "Baby On Board" car stickers; and just generally protecting their kids at every moment from everything. Have they considered large safe-deposit boxes with airholes?

These new parents have entire *lines* of safety seats, every model, a safety seat for every occasion. They order them out of their *Our Threatening Universe* magazines. Hell, our kids used to stand up in the passenger seat while we drove. (On our way to the grocery to buy sugarcoated lead paint flakes for breakfast.) The kids could stand and look outside and see things, and when it was time to stop, you, the driver, put your right arm out to keep them from hitting the windshield. It was not even federally mandated, parents did it on their own. That's what my parents and your parents did. Now we have seat belts *and* car seats *and* air bags (that sometimes do crush the children, but it's for their own good). And the kids, well, they grow up feeling restrained, withdrawn, and threatened. But child-safety experts can't quantify those things, and if they could, the safety-equipment industry couldn't sell you stuff. Like leashes for kids.

*   *   *

My son is tuh . . . tuh . . . twenty. That's tough to spit out and it's not even true. He's really twenty-two.

Jack and Jill are worried about the baby formula their kids are drinking; next they'll be concerned about sugary soft drinks; and I don't even have to worry about underage beer drinking anymore!

Not with him. It's an ongoing concern with my daughter. When you're fifty the children's questions change from "What time is *Barney* on?" to "Can we have the keg party at our house?" Actually, they don't ask. They have them when you're out of town or at the grocery store.

You return home to a spotless home after a weekend away—but over the course of the next few hours discover: an undetected beer can filled with cigarette butts behind the living-room couch or a blanket of newly fallen vomit on the bushes.

Our neighbors' kids are a little older than ours so we received a preview of what high school parties were like in this day and age. In stereo. To the right there were parties where fifteen were invited and five hundred showed up followed by police with bullhorns ordering immediate dispersal. This gets tricky because the kids always think it was you who called the police and you suddenly feel the need to enter for the witness protection program. In this particular case, however, the teenager who lived next door had to call the police herself after inviting 15 kids and having five hundred show up—like a platoon leader in 'Nam calling in an air strike on his own position when he was being overrun.

I had occasion to leave the house at 6 A.M. the next morning and witnessed the neighbor girl and her girlfriend out in their bathrobes picking up beer cans and cigarette butts from the yard before The Return of the Parents. Bedraggled and hungover, they were one of the sorriest-looking pairs I'd ever seen.

When I returned at noon, the neighbor's lawn was clean and tidy—right up to my property line, where the beer cans, cigarette butts, plastic cups, and other party detritus still covered the grass. When the parents arrived home they must have thought the Geists had some blowout.

My son developed into quite the cleaner-upper. O. J. could have used a guy like him to foil evidence technicians. (Not that the jury was interested.) The party scene was always spotless when Will was finished—but inevitably the guests left a telltale keg or cooler on the porch. I have fourteen coolers in the basement. If you need one, call me. Seriously.

To the left, the neighbors put in a swimming pool, where their high school children entertained when they were not home. Kids generally don't entertain at home during the 5 to 7 P.M. cocktail hour, but more like 11 P.M. to 3 A.M., which can disrupt sleep patterns of those on the block—not to mention one hundred feet away, where I lay tossing and turning. I called them twice and asked that they please hold it down.

I didn't want to rat them out to the cops. Not that it would help. During one of their louder parties I looked out the window and was pleased to see a police car had already arrived. But on second glance I noticed that the police officer was sitting on the pool deck drinking a beer.

By 2 A.M. this night most of the guests had passed out and only the heartiest and loudest of the revelers remained. Social Darwinism.

As it happened, I had to rise early to appear on the *CBS Sunday Morning* program (which, coincidentally, has Few-To-No teenaged viewers). I called the house a third time to ask them to tone it down. I could hear their phone ringing and hear them saying "don't answer it." And so, at 2:35 A.M.—just under three hours before I had to rise—I walked over to the pool, walked onto the diving board, and made this brief announcement: "Shuuut Uuuup!" They appeared stunned, both by the message and the messenger, who addressed the group dressed in a T-shirt and boxer shorts.

It's not easy, trying to maintain control. My son's friend, Mark, had a large third-floor bedroom where kids liked to congregate. His father tried to foil illicit activity up there by coming out of his second-floor bedroom and interdicting the flow of partygoers and party supplies. Alas, the kids were taking Outward Bound–style training in PE class, which prepared them for mountain climbing, retrieving hostages from Iran in commando raids, and reaching Mark's room.

"I'd have my eye on the stairs," his father said, "and would look out and see these ninjas hiding in the bushes and climbing up the side of our house on ropes." They hoisted kegs, too—and girls, who Mark's father would find hiding in the closet.

The teenager's will to party is powerful and unrelenting; the lust for beer unquenchable. So, on occasion, when my son was a senior, I gave in and allowed some limited "don't ask, don't tell" beer drinking in the basement when I was home. Better to be here than to be out on the highway, driving home from bars, I figured.

At the prom, my son wore a sign on his back reading "The Party Is Here," which approximately 250 friends, acquaintances, and complete strangers took as an invitation to our home for a post-prom party. My wife and I sat in the clean, quiet kitchen watching TV while hordes filled the living room, dining room, basement, porch, and yard. No one ever set foot in the kitchen. It was as if an "EBOLA VIRUS QUARANTINE" sign had been placed at the kitchen door.

When police arrived, as anticipated, I greeted the officers

myself. It wasn't easy getting through the crowd. I was fittingly obsequious, apologizing and promising to quiet things down. On the gendarmes' second visit, we actually did turn down the music and asked the kids to please be a bit quieter.

My porch resembled the Creature Cantina in *Star Wars*, elbow to elbow with strange species I'd never seen before and that science had yet to identify or give Latin names.

The third police visit was a surprise, since I felt the party had quieted down.

"It is quieter," agreed the officer. "It's the bus."

"Bus?" I replied.

"Yeh," the officer said, "there's a bus idling right under some guy's window and keeping him awake."

My God! They were coming by the *bus* load! Was there a sign for the party out on I-95? And did it say "Buses Welcome"? Were there regularly scheduled departures to my house from the Port Authority Bus Terminal?

The teenage years can be trying, but there are compensations. You don't have to get up at sunrise anymore with the little ones, change diapers, pretend you are enjoying *The Little Mermaid* the fourth time you see it, or go to the Character Breakfast at Disney World.

Vacations with teenagers are different. The kids won't even get out of the car to look at the view in Maui, for chrissake. They complain about having to leave their friends to go to a fabulous dude ranch. They put on their Walkmans and close their eyes as you drive through breathtaking Yellowstone. I forced my teenaged son to get up before dawn and go surf casting in Nantucket. It was cold and foggy and we cast for a couple of hours—with several tangled lines and lost lures, but without success—and I can still remember him calling out to me from down the beach:

"Hey, Dad!"

"Yes, Son."

"This reeeeeally sucks."

And it really did. But even things that suck can bond.

*   *   *

☞ Helpful Clip-'n'-Save Teen Party Planner ☜

Parental Status	Invitees	Projected Attendance	(Invitee / Attendee Ratio)	Party Needs
Parents home	12	4	3:1	chips
Parents may be out for evening	12	12	1:1	cups/chips
Parents away overnight	12	100+	1:10	cups/C.H.I.P.S (California Highway Patrol, or the law enforcement authority near you)
Parents away for weekend	12	500–1000	1:100	state and local authorities SWAT Team; EMT squad; Red Cross mobile disaster unit.

You will miss things like teaching them to ride bikes, rushing home to coach Little League, building little race cars for the Cub Scouts' Pinewood Derby, watching school holiday pageants, trick-or-treating with them, and attending Indian Princesses Campouts—where dads played poker and drank beer while the girls ran amok.

But now you can teach them to drive! Following my personalized course of instruction, my son had three accidents in his first few weeks of driving. (About average for guys.) Driver's training is probably best left to high school teachers, but the kids will want to start earlier than that. My daughter learned from me on our thirteen-year-old Jeep with no power steering and a stick-shift transmission that was almost completely shot. Lessons took place in vast parking lots with lots of room for error. They involved goodly amounts of laughter, whiplash, and cursing, but eventually she mastered the ornery critter, and now she'll find army tanks and eighteen-wheelers an absolute breeze.

Girls. As a little freshman, my daughter was invited to the senior prom. We told her she couldn't go, but of course she did. I waited for her date to arrive, planning to have a talk with him, man-to-man, to remind him that my daughter was but a child and would not be allowed to go to those post-prom parties that lasted all night. The doorbell rang, and when I opened the door at first I thought perhaps the porch light had burned out. But then I realized that this . . . this . . . large mammal was eclipsing the light. This was her date, a six-foot seven inch, 280-pound tackle on the football team, and I told him, in no uncertain terms, that he was to have my daughter home . . . whenever. How does three days sound? But do call if it's like over a week. OK?

With girls, there's the whole is-Angela-speaking-to-

Danielle thing all the time. And the self-esteem thing. Teenaged girls are said to be at risk of losing self-esteem. A bestseller has been written on the subject. Boys, apparently, are not at risk even though they are cut from the football and basketball teams, their teachers hate them for being disruptive, and girls won't give them the time of day until they're seniors. Some feminists came up with the annual "Take Your Daughter to Work Day" to let girls know they don't just have to grow up to be housewives who vacuum and scrub all day. I think my daughter already senses this because she won't put a glass in the dishwasher or pick up her dirty socks. I don't think these are political statements because I doubt she would really ever want a job outside the home either, thanks.

What I do to help balance the scale of self-esteem between girls and boys is this: on that special day, instead of taking my daughter to work, I just tell my son he's a worthless piece of shit.

Teenagers don't talk to you. They close their doors and get on the phone to their friends. My daughter can apparently talk on the phone even in her sleep because I hear her chatting hours after the lights go out.

When she does speak to us, certain subjects are off-limits, like anything having to do with her friends, her schoolwork, her life, herself. We are allowed into her life by honoring her requests for money and providing complimentary ground transportation to school, the mall, the movies, and her friends' houses—while terrible music blares on the radio, making conversation impossible. It could be worse. My son listened to "rap artists."

Their teenage years are difficult because you are irrelevant and unnecessary except in a chauffeur or ATM capacity. My son's friends stopped liking their parents, so he figured he had to be a little bit that way too for a while. At least that's what I like to think; the other possible explanation being that he didn't like me either—but that seems totally implausible, doesn't it?

My daughter does come out of her room—which always looks like burglars were desperately looking for something—to dine with us when the food is too tall to fit under the door. Usually she goes "ewwww!" when she sees what's being served. Her place setting includes knife, fork, spoon, and cell phone.

I, the father, can't really hug her anymore because of the breast thing, so I have to settle for a monthly peck on the cheek from the little girl who once ran to my arms at every opportunity and whom I'd happily let a cement truck run over me for.

The time will come for those Talks you need to have with teens about sex and drugs. Try to stifle the urge. They know more about sex than you do from rather explicit and detailed instruction in health class, and as one who came of age in the sixties you probably know more than you should about drugs. Don't sound too knowledgeable. These little "Just Say No" zealots will dial 1-800-ENTRAP-MOM and turn your ass in to the Narcs!

I drive by Little League games and I don't really miss all that anymore—I just miss them, my little boy and little girl. My daughter will soon be gone to college too, which is sad, although I do see a *lot* of smiles on the faces of empty nesters in the neighborhood. And besides, from what I understand, the kids these days tend to just come on back home after college anyway. They never had it so good. And neither did you.

Seven Habits of Highly Effective Parents of Teenagers

1. Pack Heat. Enhance Parental Authority with a Registered Handgun.
2. Always Say You'll Be Back in "About Ten Minutes" (Even When Leaving with Suitcases for Bermuda).
3. Monitor Mail for Arrival of Victoria's Secret and Fredericks of Hollywood Packages, as Well as Bulk Deliveries from the Trojan Corporation.
4. Set a Firm Two-Hour Study Period Each Night with No Phone Calls and No TV. (OK, How about twenty minutes? Except, of course, on nights when *90210*, *Melrose Place*, MTV, or any sports are televised.)
5. Do Not Help with Homework—At This Level It Only Lets Them Know the Depths of Your Ignorance.
6. Recognize Limitations: e.g., General Norman Schwarzkopf Couldn't Keep Beers from Teenagers.
7. Recognize Early Warning Signs of Problem Drug Use: e.g., Personnel in Blue Jackets with Yellow Letters "DEA" Rappelling Down Sides of Your Home.

OK, It's Thirteen Habits (Seven was Catchier)

8. Find a Good Auto Body Shop with "Frequent Fender" Plan.

9. When It's Time for That Little Chat About Sex, Blow It Off. (They Learn More These Days in Health Class Than You'll Ever Know.)

10. As a Warning, Keep the Name and Telephone Number of *The Cruel and Unusual Military School* on Refrigerator Door.

11. Trim Three Inches from Bottom of Teen's Bedroom Door for Passage of Messages and Meals.

12. Lie Like a Rug—About Your Own Grades, Athletic Prowess, Circle of Friends, Work Ethic and Strength of Character in Just Saying No to Beer and Pot. (It's axiomatic that your teens never meet your old friends or see yearbooks that say only "Projector Club, 2, 3" under your photo.)

13. And, Every So Often When Thinking How Completely Worthless Your Teenager Is, Compare Him or Her to Your Own Sorry Ass When You Were That Age.

College!

I usually just say that my son is "away at school," hoping people will think it's prep school. But it's not. It's college. The Family—Mom, Dad, and Sis—drove Son fourteen hours to drop him off for his freshman year of college. That is, it should have been fourteen, but it was actually more like twenty, what with Dad opting for the scenic route and stopping at tourist attractions like Dollywood and Blowing Rock, where Indians used to jump off a cliff and be lifted by mysterious winds back up to safety. My ass.

It's a wondrous thing, setting foot back on a campus. You forget you're walking around in your old-guy disguise. It feels just like it did back when you were a student, with the warm sun shining as you walk across the quad, where kids are tossing Frisbees and sunbathing. Guys are playing basketball at a frat house. Music and laughter waft from a college bar, along with the sound of bells and whistles on video games and the pinball machines that occupied most of my four—make that five—years in college. At the dorms, students are unloading U-Hauls brimming with all manner of educational materials: mini-refrigerators, stereos, CD towers, TVs, VCRs.

You stroll past an attractive coed, and lo and behold, she looks back and smiles. But wait. Not at *you*, stupid. At your son, walking alongside. Of course, of course . . .

You stop at the bookstore, where textbooks still cost twice too much and used ones are still bought back at five cents on the dollar. No, the twenty-five-thousand-dollar tuition does not include books, let alone beer, trips to and from school, fraternity dues, spring breaks, pre-spring breaks, post-spring breaks. You'll want to bring home a good fifty Gs (pretax) to pay for a year of college.

Little wonder we didn't even consider trying to save for this eventuality. Let's say I manage to save a couple grand by putting aside a few bucks each week for ten years. What the hell does that cover? Towel fees? Ray Brady, the CBS financial correspondent, had just finished airing a piece on putting money away in a special college fund when I saw him in the hallway and asked, "Now, Ray, if I put a hundred bucks in the bank now, how much will I have next month when my son leaves for college?"

I went to a state school—the University of Illinois, perennially ranked as one of the best schools in the country—where tuition for one semester (half the year) was $135. Really. So, the decision to send me to college was not all that difficult for the family. At $135, it was either send me to college or pick up the dry cleaning.

At Son's college bookstore, we bought school decals for the car. I used to think that people with college decals on their cars were really old. I still do. We also purchased sweatshirts all around. Make mine an XL. They're wearing them large these days, they shrink in the wash, and: I am fat.

We find Son's room in the dorm. It's small, of course, and done in an antebellum ('Nam) cinderblock motif that gives the place a look somewhere between Motel 6 and a minimum-security prison. But for 25K whaddaya want? The Ramada?

He meets his roommate, who seems like an OK guy, until he puts up a "Rush Is Right" bumper sticker over his desk. Could the roommate possibly be older than he looks? Like, *forty* years older? Ah, well, Son is apolitical. As long as Rush doesn't start bashing the Knicks, the two of them will get along all right I suppose.

We drive to the Target store, get two shopping carts, and make an afternoon of it. This is fun, picking out a wastebasket, a telephone, a color-coordinated extra-long phone cord, sheets, a new pillow, a desk lamp, soap, toothpaste, mouthwash, Pringles, gum—all the essentials. Mom keeps tossing packages of stationery (for all those letters home) into the cart and Son keeps putting them back. Sis tosses in Crayolas (to annoy Son) and Dad tosses in a pregnancy-test kit (for the same reason). We don't stop buying things he actually "needs"—*three* preseason football magazines?—until our two carts are overflowing. Fifty-two items. Three hundred and some bucks.

We stroll each and every walkway of the campus. The landscaping is magnificent, bespeaking the 25K. Who knows about the professors? We show Son the library (hoping it's not for the last time), and repair to an inviting Mexican restaurant that has an outdoor deck jammed with students. We buy buckets of bottled beer and sit in the sun.

Any lingering pretenses regarding Underage Drinking become instantly passé. In one fell swoop, it's gone from "Your mother and I were very disappointed to find you passed out in the shrubs again" to "How about a beer, son?"

"Thanks, Dad."

He sleeps in our hotel room with us for the last time. The

next morning we eat breakfast and go to the dorm to get his room set up. I am aware that the clock is ticking, that our hands-on parental duties are about over. For this day, and forever.

When it's time to go we stall a bit, just as we'd stalled at home, where we packed the car (basketball last), then sat on the edge of his bed for an hour looking at old photo albums, not wanting to leave, not wanting to drive him away. Summers, yes, but he would never really live with us full-time again.

I have no Hallmarkian messages to deliver to him at our parting. I have already told him that I regret having not worked harder and learned more in college. And that we love him and are proud of him.

We go down in the elevator. We stroll to the car. We hug him and kiss him good-bye. We honk and slowly pull away . . . away. I watch him in the side mirror standing completely still, watching us go.

And I remember watching him at five years old skipping off excitedly for his first day of kindergarten; and watching him out the back window at ten as he walked quickly across our backyard on a shortcut to middle school; always watching him until he completely disappeared from view. He was always disappearing, but always coming home. Until now.

Pajama
Parties

I go to parties now where
people sleep.

Men will repair to the family room after
dinner, turn on a ball game, get into La-Z-Boy easy chairs and
fall fast asleep. (Is this a Heaven's Gate sleepover or what?
Dress is casual, Nikes and a purple shroud.)

Invited to the Smiths' for dinner? Be sure to stay up late
the night before so you'll be good and tired. I'll have decaf,
Shirley, with Nutrasweet and one lump of melatonin.

When we moved to New York years ago, Jody and I wanted
to explore the downtown club scene. The cab driver deposited
us at 10 P.M. at an address that was supposed to be that of the
wild and wooly Mudd Club. But no one was there, just this
plain, unmarked steel door. There seemed to be some mistake.
I knocked. A guy opened the door, confirmed that this was indeed the Mudd Club, but that it wouldn't really be opening for
a couple more hours. "Midnight?" I gasped. "But . . . we have
a sitter."

I suppose it's all been downhill, party-wise, since then, but
in the past couple of years things have really turned grim.

I also attended a dinner party recently where the host rose

95

from the head of the table, went upstairs, and climbed into bed under the pile of guests' coats!

These narcoleptic affairs are different from those where we used to pass out from being overserved—those parties of yore where guests drank from the bottle, stuck their hands in a bag of chips, and gatored to deafening music on the dining-room floor until four A.M. No one has the energy or the drugs for that anymore. If the party was really good there might even have been a fistfight, or someone running out in a huff, or at least a little barf on the bushes.

"Parties" are different at fifty. They tend to be hormone free, smoke free, often dance free, hangover free, by invitation only, and requiring a hostess gift. I guess it's because we all have more expensive stuff to break, hard-earned stuff, like our reputations in the community.

Our capacity for alcohol is diminished and recuperation time has doubled or tripled. After an afternoon of mint juleps (straight bourbon with a rapid sugar-water delivery system) at a Kentucky Derby party, the hangover can last for up to one week! Some people our age conclude that it just isn't worth it. I shy away from such people.

It occurred to me one evening as I was crawling up my drive-way: 1. Gotta pave over this f——ing gravel! (tough on the hands) and 2. Age and alcohol don't mix!

Now that I'm 50, my Cocktail Capacity seems greatly diminished and my Hangover Longevity Time greatly increased.

You and Your Hangover—The Missing Longevity Link

After months in the lab, during which I drank exclusively from beakers and test tubes, I have developed a mathematical formula that quantifies for the first time the function of Age Longevity as a causative factor in the Hangover Longevity Time:

To determine how long your hangover recuperation will last, simply multiply:

Your Age × Your Alcohol Consumption × the A.M. Hour You Fell Asleep/Passed Out = Your Hangover Longevity in Waking Minutes.

Example One:

A 21-year-old student drinks six beers and passes out in the dorm at 2 A.M. Saturday night.

The Hangover Time is $21 \times 6 \times 2 = 252$ Waking Minutes.

The student awakens at noon and feels like hell until 4:12 P.M. Sunday afternoon.

Example Two:

A 50-year-old drinks six beers and goes home at 2 A.M.

The Hangover Time is $50 \times 6 \times 2 = 600$ Waking Minutes.

The 50-year-old awakening at noon would feel like hell until 10 P.M., or all day Sunday.

Example Three:

A 50-year-old drinks four martinis and passes out on the host's toilet at 2 A.M.

(Note: beer is a factor of 1×; wine 2×; mixed drinks 3×; martinis 4×; grain alcohol, Sterno, Prestone 5×)

The Hangover Time is $50 \times (4 \times 4) \times 2 = 1,600$ Waking Minutes.

Our 50-year-old is hungover until . . . Tuesday.

Note: This study presupposes an aspirin, greasy cheeseburger, and Bloody Mary intervention program to ameliorate symptoms, and No Regurgitation. (Dry heaves OK.)

Parties now revolve around food. Canapés, hors d'oeuvres, buffet dinners, full-blown sit-down dinners. All in all, we'd rather eat. Have a cup of decaf. Call it a night. Golf date at eight.

Other than parties where you eat, social life pretty much involves going out to eat. On a recent restaurant outing, the other couple drove us home at 11:15, Saturday night. "Want to come in for a drink?" we asked. "Nah," they said. Maybe it was for the best. Mexican food and all. Prop the window and go to bed early.

Except . . . these were part of our Wild Bunch, who just two years ago were gatoring, and dropping trou on our dining-room table, and swimming in their tuxedos! The bottom falls out fast, at fifty.

Eating becomes the prime social activity on Saturday night, and remains so from this day forward, through the (early) evenings at the Del Ray Beach Sizzler and the Phoenix Red Lobster, right on through to the Last Supper. Digestion becomes late-night entertainment: belching and farting in the car on the moonlit drive home. (Don't scrimp on power windows.)

Other than estate-planning seminars, the other big social activity is going out to the movies, although this is not always easy in the suburbs, where a tenplex is likely to carry four

Schwarzenegger films, three Van Dammes, two Stallones, and a Chuck Norris.

We could go out to dinner *and* a movie, but if we go to the late show (9:35) can we stay awake? And doesn't theater popcorn *kill* you or something? And the drinks are too big. And popcorn and a Coke costs, like, twenty-three bucks.

And there is always the danger that we've seen the movie before and won't realize it until ten minutes after it begins.

Wilding

Completely Out-of-Control Saturday Night Out for 50-Year-Olds

- Take family van WITHOUT the passenger-side air bag! Go on!
- Play *Tesh Lets Loose* tape a notch too loudly for other three people in the van.
- Blow into restaurant at 6:37 for a 6:30 reservation. Let the chips fall where they may!
- Ask for table "sort of near" the smoking section. Continue to breathe normally.
- Order your usual light beer *and* regular beer and mix fifty-fifty!
- Decline imported bottled water, and drink TAP water! You've always been a rebel.
- Order red meat! A burger WITH cheese! Throw lactose intolerance to the winds.
- Vegetarian in the group orders stir fry and says, "DON'T hold the MSG"! Prepare to trip out.
- Order chicken with the skin ON!
- Order "Seaman's Platter"—Fried! Are you on acid!?

- Regale table with time you went to the beach and used SPF4! No way!
- Order a DESSERT (with four spoons). Completely zany.
- Get half decaf, HALF CAF! Feel the buzz!
- On the way home break out a pack of SUGARLESS gum!
- Crank Yanni on the Blaupunkt.
- Drop Altoids.

Up with Codgers

Do Not Despair, Fellow Quintenarians!

That is the appealing and highly marketable message put forth in a spate of new books extolling the joys of aging.

The most renowned of these is Gail Sheehy's uplifting bestseller *New Passages,* in which she celebrates "The Flaming Fifties" and makes us all feel better by redefining middle age as fully 60–75 years old! (Thanks, Gail.) Ms. Sheehy contends that growing older means "becoming better, stronger, deeper, wiser, funnier, freer, sexier. . . ."

After careful reading and thorough consideration, I have reached the conclusion that Ms. Sheehy is full of shit on this subject.

The only "new passages" my aging friends are experiencing involve the increasingly involuntary passage of gas, passage of the occasional kidney stone, or passage into The Great Beyond.

Ms. Sheehy transforms a seven-word bumper sticker, "You're Not Getting Older, You're Getting Better," into a 498-page volume. Not since *Seven Habits of Highly Effective People* and Saddam's invasion of Kuwait has such unwarranted expansionism occurred.

"I wish I had a penny," she writes, "for every post-menopausal wild girl who's told me she's off to track gorillas in the Congo without her husband, or she's setting off with another woman friend to climb mountains, or she's resuscitated her tennis game and is now entering tournaments."

Personally I'd want a dime. But that's because I'm so infrequently in the company of unaccompanied Congo gorilla trackers—at least the post-menopausal ones (and do you dare ask?). She goes on to hail all of our aging comrades who ". . . write and perform poetry, take up the marimba, enter politics." Again, it seems like a fairly select group.

I, personally, would be better off with a penny for every friend who's visiting their kid in the county juvenile detention center, undergoing quadruple bypass surgery, or filing for bankruptcy.

New Passages is chock-full of throw-pillow aphorisms like "Let's replace 'ageing' with 'sageing' "; and it includes some nice graphic elements, like that chart showing how 60–75 is now middle age.

Was Prozac mentioned at all in the acknowledgments? Could she be suffering from the dreaded Kathy Lee Gifford syndrome? Gail cannot stop coming up with euphemistic labels. She would have made an outstanding social director on the *Titanic:* Tweet! "Time for a fun impromptu evening splash party. Everybody in the water!" Or perhaps one of those real estate ad writers who describes a house as not so much "Under the Expressway" as it is "Convenient to Transportation."

She describes the period between 45 and 65 as a second

adolescence—"Middlessence"—and except for obligations and responsibilities and health problems and no dating and estate planning seminars instead of wild parties and professional concerns (like having a job) she's absolutely right! (Her "middlessence" is my "pre-deceased.")

"Middlessence" is her label for this period, but hardly the only one. Not only does Gail have labels for everything, she often has two or three. Or four.

"Find your passion," she preaches, and hers is clearly labeling things. She can't seem to stop herself. She's like a night stockboy at Wal-Mart.

Gail also labels this "Middlessence" period "Second Adulthood."

And she goes on to label it "The Age of Mastery." And "The Vietnam Generation." And for good measure she labels the middle part "The Flaming Fifties." Gail! Stop it.

Her "Flaming Fifties" are followed by her "Serene Sixties"—especially serene for millions of what she might call The "Delightfully Deceased" in that age group. "The Serene Sixties" are followed by her "Sage Seventies"; the "Nobility of the Nineties"; and those "Celebratory Centenarians."

Gail does allow as how "for some of us time will run out before we can really engage or enjoy the second half" of our lives, but don't let that get you down. Deal with it. Slap some smiley-face stickers on that coffin. Her three bestsellers, *Passages*, *The Silent Passage*, and now *New Passages*, should certainly be followed by *Final Passage*.

There is her World War II Generation; the Silent Generation; the aforementioned Vietnam Generation (born 1946–55); the Me Generation (1956–65); and the Endangered Generation (1966–80). She keeps the generations short—9-year-old mothers?!—because she has all these damned labels to use up. If she had to lick all these labels *she'd* be gagging, not us.

Within these packages wrapped up so neatly and completely in labels are—guess what?—more labels, such as "Save Your Life Wives" and "Start Over Dads." She likes that last group, men like Frank Gifford, who had a child at 59 (and whose faculties had apparently already begun to deteriorate when he decided with whom he would start over). Clint Eastwood at 63, Norman Lear in his seventies. Gail likes them because they have time to be "fully nurturant co-parents." Aieeee! Talk like that is enough to send deadbeat dads scurrying to Vegas to consort with bimbos and to throw the tuition money on craps tables.

She may not quite *get* men in middlessence. She goes on and on about women growing older and better while her men are balding and becoming sexually impotent. She admonishes men to take up gardening instead of chasing young women and playing competitive sports. My hydrangea is bigger and more upright than yours!

A companion in all this is Betty Friedan, who writes "It is as obsolete a mystique in 1994 to describe age as the deterioration of youth as it was in 1954 to describe a woman as only a mother and wife"—except, Betty, age is not an attitude—it's real. It's on your driver's license. I can see Betty now, wandering through the cemetery inspiring people to get up and go on with their lives.

Meanwhile Gail goes right on labeling things: "The Samson Complex" and "The Sexual Diamond" and "The Meanings Crisis" and "The Age of Integrity" and . . .

All right, Gail, FREEZE! Put down that labeling gun! Nice and easy. . . . Are you a victim of Obsessive-Compulsive Labeling Syndrome, or is the caps lock button on your keyboard just stuck?

"Let me put a question to you," Gail asks. "Will your personal life story in second adulthood be conceived as a progress story or a decline story?"

And let me put a question to you, Gail: who cares if the glass is half empty or half full, when your teeth are in it?

Taxi
& Takeoff

**Twelve-Step "Butt Bunny Hop and Double Pump"
Program for Fifty-Year-Olds Attempting to Exit
Taxicabs Unassisted**

1. Perform series of "Butt Bunny Hops," Pushing Down with Hands to Lift Buttocks and Shifting Raised Buttocks Toward Curbside Door.
2. Unlatch Door and Push Outward.
3. Torque Body and Swing Outside Leg Out the Door.
4. Grab Back of Front Seat and Plant Outside Foot on Pavement.
5. Dig Outside Elbow into Seat and Grab Top of Cab Door Frame with Inside Hand. (Inform driver you'll be out shortly.).
6. Begin "Double Pump" Action by Rocking Forward . . .
7. Then Lunging Backward . . .
8. And Thrusting Entire Body Upward in One Burst!
9. Expel Air from Lungs in Loud Grunting Sound (Employed by Powerlifters).

10. Grab Top of Cab Door.
11. Stand and Tuck in Shirttail Using Opened Door to Conceal Yourself from Passersby.
12. Close door.

Food
(Only Fit)
for Thought

*A*t 50, everyone is always riding your butt about what you're eating. "You can't eat this, you can't eat that . . ." It's usually the damned Center for Science in the Public Interest. First they denounced killer fettuccine Alfredo. (Mmmmm!) Then it was killer moo goo gai pan, then killer movie popcorn, now: Killer Tacos! The CSPI says an order of beef and cheese nachos has as much fat as 10 Dunkin Donuts—glazed! And the nachos are an appetizer. The chile relleno dinner that follows has as much fat as 27 slices of bacon. Hay Caramba! We get the message: If you eat, you die. Fine. Why don't you guys at the CPSI start *eating* dinner and stop sending it to the crime lab?

When we eat out we're supposed to order those menu items with the little red hearts next to them that signify healthfulness. I appreciate those little hearts. I always have a tough time deciding what to order and the little hearts allow me to quickly rule out those menu items as completely unsatisfying.

When I order at restaurants the waiters sometimes think I must be crying out for help. If I wrote down my orders they'd be considered suicide notes.

A colleague once looked at my breakfast plate and gasped: "What is this, a cholesterol testing station?" Nooo, it is eggs and bacon and buttered toast—exactly what my high school health class teachers told me to eat.

Night before last in Topeka, I had delicious barbecued rib tips. As an appetizer. My entrée was a 16-ounce Kansas City strip steak and a baked potato with butter, sour cream, chives, bacon bits, Cheddar cheese, and plenty of salt and pepper. I did have a green salad, but smothered it in a blanket of creamy blue cheese dressing. My beverage item was a vodka martini straight up with three olives. I had a refill. The time was 11 P.M. It was so good I had the same thing last night. I am alive as of this writing.

At 50, this is stupid, I know, but life's good while it lasts. So many things are not good these days. It's not that they taste bad, they just don't taste at all. My brother-in-law is always making tofu-burgers and insisting they taste the same as real ones. At Thanksgiving dinner he serves a vegetable casserole and regales the family with tales of the "starch rot and protein putrification" going on inside our bodies. He takes me to health food stores where everybody is pale and thin and lackluster and engaged in conversations about their colon cleansers. Yikes. The white-haired guy behind the counter says DHEA is great stuff. "I started taking it two weeks ago," he says, "when I turned 40." 40!? I thought he was a healthy-looking *eighty*-year-old.

My own house is stocked with all manner of tasteless foods. Instead of good 'n' greasy potato chips, we have the new baked Tostitos. They're the worst. Ever make paper in grade school? Same thing. We have Healthy Choice soup, which is fine if you add enough salt. We have lite bread so thin I have to make two pieces of toast at once—sort of a butter sandwich. We have skim milk, which even the cat won't accept. Won't eat the poached fish either that I put down for her after I don't eat it.

Poached fish is *really* good for you, and it tastes like water. Most fish taste like the water. A few years back, steak joints began closing—as if Eliot Ness were working for the CPSI—and were replaced by more healthful fish restaurants. Because most fish have no taste, these restaurants would blacken them, squirt lemon juice on them, and drown them in heavy cream sauces. Of course you could do the same thing to a pair of socks and not have to deal with the bones. You'd see on the menu a "Grilled, Smoked, and Peppered Mackerel with Arugula and Endive." They were doing everything to these fish but putting them in lipstick and spiked heels.

I have learned to eat fish—reluctantly—because they have finally learned to lend them taste. I like some sushi, probably because of the pasty rice, soy sauce, hot wasabe, and ginger. Grilled salmon is good because it is grilled. Grilled Dr. Scholl's shoe liners are probably also good.

I don't know my cholesterol level. I had it checked once in a pharmacy and it was 201, but a lot of gravy and mashed potatoes have flowed under the bridge since.

That was in Sausalito, California, where there are street signs proclaiming the place a "Cholesterol Free Zone." Sounded like something Rod Serling dreamed up. The trendy Marin County community has also declared itself a Nuclear Free Zone—and there hasn't been a detonation since. You'd have heard about it.

I saw a man on the street there carrying a suspicious-looking brown bag and asked him what was in it. "It's a large cheeseburger laden with cholesterol," the young man answered with a smirk. "And fries." If I'd had a blackjack I'd have worked the punk over. I told a cop, but no arrest was made.

"First, the ice cream parlor developed a cholesterol-free ice cream," explained Fred Mayer, the local pharmacist who started the Cholesterol Free Zone movement. "Then, the cookie store introduced a low-cholesterol oatmeal cookie and the pizza parlor followed with a cholesterol-free pizza."

They leave out the cheese. "It's called foccacia," explained a guy at the pizza parlor named Chris. Forgotzia cheese.

Sausalito's fat-free fundamentalists were lining up with me at the pharmacy to check their cholesterol levels, flocking to sushi bars, and doing their weekly grocery shopping at health food stores where all things bran jumped off the shelves—although certain health foods continued to meet resistance, like the tofu and spinach hot dogs. Green hot dogs. I was trained not to eat green hot dogs.

There is a resistance movement. Fred's Place restaurant is a rallying point for the underground animal fat purists who refuse to knuckle under to these clean artery types.

They served me one of Fred's specialties. "This is the Swedish breakfast," explained the waitress. "Whole wheat toast topped with chocolate cake (!) with melted cheese topped with three eggs over medium with grilled onions and a side of hash browns." Jesus, why weren't customers just falling dead off their stools?!

A bit heavy for you? Then try the french toast made with egg bread soaked in pancake batter made with vanilla ice cream, then grilled, then deep-fat-fried to perfection. Murder incorporated.

George Richardson took over Fred's Place, vowing to preserve it as a cholesterol cathedral. "We're an outlet for those that want to be good most of the time but when they wanna be bad, really bad, they know where to go." Pharmacist Fred Mayer himself admits to sneaking over to Fred's place twice a week.

A man who eats here regularly and appears to have made it to 50 years of age or so (although I suppose he could be 30) says he loves the food and that he brings in his little dog, Earl, to lick the platters clean. Shouldn't the ASPCA know about this?

Other Sausalito restaurants are all adding lots of new low and no cholesterol items to their menus such as tofu burgers and poached fish.

And will George be making any menu changes at Fred's?

"We're gonna definitely drop the salad," he vows.

I know what we're supposed to order. Free-range chicken—skinned. When I see free-range chicken on a menu, the first thing that comes to mind is a flock of chickens bounding chee-tahlike across Montana. The second thing that comes to mind is: "*Twenty-five bucks* for a free-range chicken dinner?!" When chickens stayed home, they were five and a quarter.

Some skeptics claim free-range chicken is stringier, tougher, and more gamey, and that gallivanting around out there makes them susceptible to all sorts of worms and parasites and infections—sort of like having a free-range boyfriend.

Menus also trumpet new "hormone-free, stress-free beef." I like knowing my beef is drug-free, and pray it never drank or smoked. As for "stress-free," some New Age ranchers are naming their cows and keep them together in peer groups to make them happier, and one rancher went so far as to ban artificial insemination. You can imagine the celebration in the barn that night! Another says he picks the happiest-looking cow as the next one to slaughter, which must make for the sourest-looking herd you ever saw.

Menus are also sporting "natural grain-fed catfish," raised in the "pure air and pure waters" of Mississippi—fish that have passed the exacting examinations of The Catfish Institute. I like knowing the educational background of my meal.

Brunch menus are carrying the new, miracle low-cholesterol egg—although serious questions have been raised about the ability of chickens to even *lay* such eggs. It's asking a lot on short notice. You can imagine the chickens talking amongst themselves in the coop after work: "Boss calls me into his office and tells me to start layin' low-cholesterol eggs. I says, 'Jeez, boss, you're killin' us out there! You already got us doin' small, medium, large, extra-large. Whaddya want out of us for chrissake? Pastels for Easter?!'"

Ideal Weight Chart for Fiftyish Females/Males

Clip and affix this to the refrigerator door and kiss so-called weight problems goodbye forever. (And, yes, all weights listed are for human beings.)

Height	Small boned	Medium boned	Large boned
5'0"	180 lbs.	200 lbs.	250+ lbs.
5'6"	225 lbs.	250 lbs.	300+ lbs.
+6'0"	250 lbs.	300 lbs.	400+ lbs.

Using this system to calculate your own exact personal ideal weight, simply take your current weight and add 8 pounds.

Fifties
Fashion

Belts are posing a fashion predicament for male boomers: where to wear it? Over the protruding gut? Under the gut? Or, all around the gut?

Some men, like myself, are determined to stay the course, and we continue belting the same way we always have, directly around our waists. This, however, means continually buying bigger and bigger belts ("Would you like to put this on your Coach Preferred Belt Customer charge card, sir?"). This is expensive, humiliating, and demoralizing. The price for trying to stay too long with an old belt, however, is pain.

The least attractive option is to wear the belt "high on the hog," so to speak, or above the belly. This has the unfortunate effect of: 1. Making you look like the recording secretary of your high school ham radio club; 2. Making your pants too short (Clam Digger Syndrome); and 3. Making it appear that you are a safety nut who's surgically implanted a Personal Air Bag.

The option I see most "middle-aged" men opting for now is the "truck-stop style," i.e., wearing the belt low-slung, below the waist. This has a curious effect. Over time, as the belly balloons, the buckle begins facing downward, ever more southward, under increasing pressure from a glacier of fat. The "Gut Gradient," as measured by the "Buckle Tilt Angle," first becomes noticeable at about fifteen degrees and will in some cases reach forty-five degrees or more. In pronounced cases of keg-sized beer guts, researchers have actually had to stoop down to record the angle.

Giorgio Armani has proclaimed fashion "dead," saying boomers dictate the market and we've moved beyond a need for high style: "Clothes that promote sexual attraction and reproduction"—crotchless underwear?—"are fundamentally different than those that suit cocooning and reaching maturity in a career or relationship."

So where the hell did this new national abdominal muscle fetish come from, with the accompanying fashion rage for short, bare-midriff shirts and blouses, designed to show off those killer, washboard, six-pack abs?

Fat chance. I'm fighting that current fashion tide, going the other way, finding my own look, my own style, which is more a long-tailed shirt thing—untucked. Call it casual concealment. (It's a more natural look than trying to wear a cummerbund with jeans and a casual shirt—or with a swimsuit.)

I found if I wore an untucked plaid J. Crew shirt and carried a skateboard around with me, the loose, baggy look almost started to make sense.

Still, people know you're hiding something. Store detectives will stop you. And, men, if you let your hair get too long (especially if you tie it back in a ponytail), be prepared for women to smile warmly at you and purr: "Awwww . . . what's your due date?"

Eventually, the untucked thing wasn't working for me anyway. It was sort of OK, kind of jaunty and devil-may-care, wearing the untucked polo shirt around on weekends. But during the week, an untucked white shirt with a suit and tie at the office was not happening—not even on Dress Down Fridays. It makes you look . . . drunk.

"Why don't you get those Sans-A-Belt elastic waist slacks?" Jody asked. I refrained from striking her (you have to work at a relationship) and replied: "Ed McMahon wears 'em." She accepted that.

The best I've looked lately, I think, was giving a commencement speech. Although everyone knows you're old and dull or you wouldn't *be* a commencement speaker, you get to wear a cap and gown, which I found surprisingly flattering. Could be a fashion trend: Commencement Wear for every occasion. The black color is slimming, and the long, flowing style affords our wearer a touch of grace and concealment all the way down to the shoes! Think "Moo-Moo Formal." In addition, the commencement gown is a youthful look (normally worn by students), and it allows you to wear black well into June.

Eventually, concealment may give way to out-and-out camouflage clothing, in which the observer cannot quite make out where you end and your immediate environment begins. It works well in the military to avert enemy sniper fire, and it might just do the same for catty, sniping remarks.

Try wearing Vietnam camouflage fatigues to outdoor barbecues; floral prints to garden parties; Operation Desert Storm fatigues to the beach. Entertaining at home? Have that favorite chair re-covered, make yourself an outfit from the same fabric, sit in that chair—and don't move.

Sometimes wearing black and avoiding strong horizontals is simply not enough.

But you know . . . they do make . . . *girdles* for men. Not real men, of course. Soft, flabby modern men like myself—who are saying, "Diet and exercise? Sacrifice and pain? Screw this, I'll just buy myself a . . . a . . ."

But it sticks in their craw; we can't say the word. Neither can women. Women now call corsets and girdles "shapewear." Marketers know this.

So they're calling the men's girdle the Man Band. It's a nylon and spandex band that slims the stomach and love handles. Call me Nancy, but if it comes in flesh tones, screw it indeed, I'll never diet or exercise again. Eighteen bucks. One time.

The Man Band is by designer Nancy Ganz, who came out with a line of women's undergarments years ago that shaped breasts, butts, and thighs. "Women want to take control," she explained, cosmically. Control of their butts, I guess. She called the line BodySlimmers.

Men bought them! No, not real men. But not just your Ru Pauls either. Modern men. The Smoothie Waist Eliminator was popular in the larger sizes.

So Nancy Ganz introduced this Man Undercover Collection that "reconfigures the male anatomy." (That's where you get terms like "dick-head." Reconfiguration.)

In addition to the Man Band, she brought out:

- The Ab Fab Cincher Tank—a tank top with a hidden Lycra panel that slims the stomach. A Lycra panel.
- The Double Agent Boxer—$30 underpants with discreet nylon-Lycra panels.
- The Butt Booster for Men—lifts, gives greater dimension, and enhances.

119 Bill Geist

Now, if *my* ass gets any more enhancement I'll have to put a red flag on it before I drive on the highway.

She was really smart to introduce these corrective garments on the QVC shopping network so guys didn't have to stand in line with them at the store. It's as bad as buying Trojans as a teenager used to be; you know, when the clerk bellowed: "Lubricated or Non-lubricated?" (See, young fellows, back then it used to be illegal for a minor to buy condoms; now you get a letter of commendation from President Clinton—who also asks if you'd mind sharing your partner's phone number.)

My Hammacher Schlemmer catalogue offers "Slenderizing Manshape Undergarments . . . specially designed to slim your shape and help clothes fit more smoothly."

And there are the popular Super Shaper Briefs for men, which are Lycra spandex underwear with padding in the rear to provide a more toned, muscular look. They are also said to be great for making bicycle rides and lengthy sermons easier on the butt.

The Super Shapers promise "eye-catching buttocks" and "pumped-up muscular buns," utilizing sewn-in pads and a center seam for cleavage.

"This is a body part that can't be built up through exercise," a spokesman explains, although I'm not so sure about that. By eating a high-protein, high-carbohydrate, high-fat diet, and constantly utilizing my ass in the home and at the office, I've built mass, definitely, and may not need the product.

However, if you order one and enclose an extra five bucks you also receive the "snap-in, fly-front Endowment Pad" that enhances the wearer. You know, down there, in front. This was perhaps inspired by Acapulco beach boys who pioneered in this dicknology by stuffing dinner rolls in their bikini-brief swimsuits. Of course they couldn't go in the water or they'd have soggy dough running down their legs. Ish. A spokesperson for Super Shaper claims 80 percent of the customers order the endowment pad. The pads are not sold separately. I asked. As journalists must.

The same company also sells the Elyse Pad-A-Panty for women, and I think they also market "Lipo-Slim Briefs," which I saw advertised in an airline magazine. They claim these briefs cause you to lose weight just by wearing them. They "*were* $69.00" but "*now*" they're "just $19.95" (if you buy size small, but who buys size small briefs for fat people?).

How do the briefs *do* this? Easy. The briefs simply "dissolve fat and hydric deposits" with "thousands of thermo-active micropore cells." Idiot. Accepting the offer gives you the privilege of purchasing forty bucks' worth of thigh cream—great in lattes!—for just $4.95, as well as a $20 diet book for just $9.95 entitled *The More You Eat, the More You Lose.* Shipping and handling is absolutely free, although "delivery" is extra. One thing confused me: the "Before" and "After" pictures for the briefs were the same ones used for another product, the Elyse Body Toner, advertised in the same magazine. Must have been identical twins.

The Ridgewood Corset Shop in my hometown doesn't carry girdles for men, yet. "This idea will take a little while to get to Middle America," said a spokesperson for the clothing line. "But it will."

Meanwhile, the Ridgewood Corset Shop is having the last laugh. Its name was, and is, outmoded. (The store sponsored Little League teams that just hated having "Ridgewood Corset Shop" emblazoned across the backs of their uniforms.) Its product line seemed hopelessly outmoded too, as we boomers moved earlier through the all-natural, let-it-all-hang-out phase. We could do it, then. Now if we let it all hang out, it drags on the ground. Business is booming at the Ridgewood Corset Shop—and no one is burning their Wonderbra.

The Wonderbra is a wonder of engineering design, sold by the Sara Lee company. They say "Nobody Doesn't Like Sara Lee," and now we know why.

Women stood in line for those. Cleavage, decolletage, and bodacious ta-tas are back in fashion, (black-tie charity balls these days look like lunchtime at Hooters), excavated by plunging necklines, uplifted by miracle fabrics. But why the bust boom now? A recent article attributed the trend to a "conservative tide that has brought back old-fashioned values promoting the family and a traditional stay-at-home lifestyle." Stay home and what? Watch Mom dance in her Wonderbra on the coffee table?

Or could it be that we're all getting, you know, fatter, which is not what you like to see on the bottom, but can be gangbusters up top. (Alas, this does not hold true for men, whose tits are also growing larger as we age.)

Nails, like tits, have likewise become important fashion statements. Nails don't age. You don't have to put them on a diet or do nail exercises. They can dazzle and draw attention away from bodily problem areas.

For a small weekly maintenance fee, your nails can look as good as or better than those of some wrinkle-free, slim-hipped bitch in her twenties.

"People get off their deathbeds to come in here and have their nails done," Joyce Sanders tells me. She is the proprietor of the Hair & Nail Shack, in Tolar, Texas, a town of 359 people that has no bank, no drugstore, not even a police officer—yet it has five places to get your nails done. "A manicure is as important to people around here as toothpaste," she says. "They come in here with a 104 or a 105 temperature before they'll go to a doctor. They come in half dead." Makes sense, really. I mean, what if you croaked and had to lie in state with your chipped nails folded across your chest while hundreds of mourners walked by?

There are now approximately 27,000 nail emporiums in America employing about 185,000 "nail technicians" who perform manicures, pedicures, nail wraps, nail extensions, and a Louvre-load of nail art: fourteen-karat-gold nail charms, nail feathers, family photos, nail diamonds, nail birthstones, nail chains, nail foil coverings, nail lace, and purple snakeskin fingernail covers, among other things. Some nail techs make emergency house calls. Doctors do not. It is a changing America.

Tight
Tux Tips

A tuxedo is a cruel indica-
tor of male weight gain. It's something you
wear relatively infrequently, and "Substantial Girth Changes May Occur" from one New Year's Eve
party or one wedding to the next.

Particularly since, who goes to weddings anymore, or for
that matter, who goes out on New Year's Eve? I'm usually at
home, un-tuxed, trying to figure out how to tape the big ball
drop in Times Square so we can hit the damned sack.

With a tux, there's never any time left for corrective action,
because you're always putting it on ten minutes before it's time
to leave. And that's when you discover: the jacket is too tight,
through the shoulders and across the belly, so you'll have to
spend the evening with your jacket unbuttoned—and without
raising your hands too high or you'll rip out the armpits. (That
flamenco thing you do with the castanets is out!)

The shirt is so tight in the neck that the top button pops
off; not to mention you can never find those damned shirt studs.
The glue gun is the only answer at this late date. If Martha
Stewart can make a *station wagon* with a glue gun surely you
can fasten your shirt.

And the pants! My God, not even close. You've picked up at least an inch since you wore them last year and they probably shrank another inch when you were overserved and went in the swimming pool with your tux on and tried to do a synchronized-swimming routine with the hostess (whom you'd pushed in earlier—and what *was* her name and why don't they ever call anymore?).

What to do? You can't just slip on some green Dockers with the tux jacket.

Ten-Step Emergency Procedure for Too-Tight Tux Trousers

1. Number one, empty bladder to help deflate midsection.
2. Number two, number two wouldn't hurt either.
3. Remove bulky wallet, hip flask, etc. from pockets
4. Cut legs off wife's control-top panty hose. Wear.
5. Lie on back.
6. Inhale deeply.
7. Hold.
8. Pull up zipper with pliers as high as possible.
9. Wrap midsection with duct tape (half roll).
10. Cover this entire project with a large cummerbund.

Most
Traumatic
Swimsuit
Syndrome

*J*ust when women thought they'd experienced in childbirth the worst pain they'd ever know, it's time to buy a swimsuit. Women never seem to think they look as good as they should in swimsuits, although I've never asked Kathy Ireland how she thinks she looks in the *Sports Illustrated* swimsuit issue. (That's cute, the way they call it a "swimsuit" issue. You can just hear all those hockey and boxing and football fans commenting: "a bit too long waisted . . . cute print . . . too structured . . . the extra seam is nice . . . strong color for her, but I would have gone with the puce." Fine.)

Even my tall, modelesque teenaged daughter tries on about thirty suits before finding one she thinks she looks acceptable in. Customer satisfaction gradually declines in the swimsuit department until motherhood, then often takes a precipitous nosedive, before continuing its inexorable descent throughout the 40s and bottoming out around 50. At some point after that the customer no longer gives a good goddamn.

I skip town on a business trip when my wife says she's going shopping for a new swimming suit—a survival reflex like diving away from a live grenade.

I used to go with her, and this is my advice to other men: 1. Don't. 2. Ever. 3. But if you must, pack a lunch as well as an after-school snack, because by "middle age" the quixotic quest for a semi-flattering swimsuit can involve three malls, seven stores, two states, and three dozen try-ons. 4. Wear shades. This way, willowy 22-year-olds won't catch your wanton stares, and swollen matrons can't see the stark terror in your eyes that even a skirted suit cannot erase.

These days Jantzen and the others are offering bathing suits that look more like ball gowns—and about as revealing as suits worn by hazardous-material response teams. (Both protect from toxic sights.) Not that men look any better. I often wish I could borrow my wife's one-piece. It's all so sad; we used to pack sandwiches for the beach, and now everybody we see there is so gross, who can eat?

For the record, Jody is not at all Rubenesque, just self-critical. We all see ourselves as ten years younger than we are, until we try on bathing suits. She still sees herself in a swimsuit as that 20-year-old finalist in the college Dolphin Queen pageant, which she was. I still see myself in jeans as a James Dean type, when Jimmy Dean pork sausage is more like it.

"Ugh!" Jody cries from the dressing room. "This is horrible. Horrible!" I ask the attendant if there are any sharp objects in the dressing-room area. She doesn't think so. Pencils? Why? Suicide notes.

Salespeople say a woman's swimsuit search may begin optimistically, in the two-piece department, but that things quickly become complicated as women jump back and forth between the Petite and the Lane Bryant racks, picking out tops and bottoms, respectively. From there the journey continues into the one-piece department and on to the Super Spandex aisle, where ultra-elastics probably developed by NASA to slingshot astronauts into orbit have now been adapted for use in the swimsuit industry.

These high-tech contraptions squeeze globs of fatty tissue up and away from the abdominal area and out the top of the suit, where it's the wearer's job to reconfigure that tissue mass into two separate, distinct, and reasonably proportional breasts. (Note to Buyers: these gripping garments will greatly increase your cup size and, in rare cases, hat and shoe size as well.)

For the longest time the stop of last resort for milady was the Back Yard Pool & Patio Shoppe, where an XXXL could try on one of those plastic aboveground swimming pools by easing her head through the drain hole before heading off to that big splash party.

Now, thanks to DuPont laboratories, there is a new generation of swimsuits that has adopted control-top pantyhose principles and offers real hope to bulging boomers.

There is the Miraclesuit, which promises you'll look ten pounds thinner in thirty seconds; the Slimsuit, promising to reduce your waistline by an inch or two; Lands' End's Slender Suit; Sears's Slim Allure; and Kathy Ireland's own line at Kmart. (Kathy's has no tummy control panel, but, then, what the hell would she know about such things?)

The new suits are marvels of structural engineering, with padded bras, extra seams, underwires, thick "power panels" in the torso area, elastic bands, darts, and straps. And they're marvels of optical illusion, too, with features like high-cut hips to give the impression of longer legs, and lots of ruffles and bright colors around the bust that shout: "Yoo-hoo! Look! Not down there, up here!" Some just give up and throw a little skater skirt over the whole mess.

Most of them are loaded with spandex (the Official Fabric of the Boomer Generation). With up to three times the normal dosage of spandex, the suits fit tighter than body condoms, and come with special instructions on how to get them on. (Roll them on, like panty hose—and condoms.) To exhale in one of these suits is to break your ribs, and once wet they cannot be removed. If you have to visit the rest room, just hope there's someone around with a Swiss army knife.

Spandex is the lazy person's answer to muscle tissue. The more spandex in the suit the more support, they say, and God knows we all need lots of support to go to the beach these days: physical, emotional, spiritual.

Today, spandex is in everything: pants, shirts, underwear. I think it's on breakfast menus in California. This miracle fabric—with three times the restraining power of rubber!—was invented in 1958 by DuPont scientist John Shivers. We owe him much.

The next generation of Dupont's Lycra spandex is Lycra Soft, which a company spokesperson says will be used in underwear designed for and aimed at the gravity-stricken baby-boomer market. The spokesperson says many of the older boomers are giving up on diets and exercise—"putting their fate in their underpants." Has it not always been so?

Cutlery

*I*t is believed by some in the scientific community that following a nuclear holocaust the only living things remaining on planet Earth will be cockroaches and Cher.

Baby boomers are flocking to plastic surgeons. Some are fighting 50, some are fighting 40, a few are fighting 35, says Dr. Elliott Jacobs, a plastic surgeon who had a little work done himself as he closed in on the Big 5–O.

"Got rid of my double chin and my love handles," he says. "50 was very traumatic. The golden age, the beginning of the slippery slope. My son now beats me at squash. I'm a card-carrying member of the AARP! It's only eight bucks."

It used to be that the vast majority of plastic surgery clients were over 50; now the vast majority are under 50. Does this necessarily mean that baby boomers are more vain than preceding generations? Why, yes. Yes it does. Of we boomers, psychiatrist Harold Bloomfield observes, "This group was somehow programmed to never get older—that sets us up for a whole series of disappointments." He sees an increase in a once rare condition called dysmorphophobia, the intense but unfounded fear of looking ugly.

More than one million "aesthetic surgery operations" were performed last year, according to the American Academy of Cosmetic Surgery, with liposuction and eyelid jobs leading the way. Dr. Jacobs was hard at work in his office on Park Avenue in New York performing all manner of augmentations, reductions, implantations, corrections, and nips and tucks on scalps, foreheads, noses, eyes, ears, chins, throats, breasts, bellies, hips, thighs, and calves. Dr. Jacobs's liposuction machine whirs incessantly these days.

On a December day his office was as busy as Santa's workshop. (Johnny wants a lid job; Susie needs new breasts.) "People want to look their best for holiday parties," he says between operations. "And a lot of patients are going on cruises or trips south." Some stop by on their way to the airport for a few hundred dollars' worth of collagen shots, which remove wrinkles in a matter of hours.

Cosmetic surgeons now get emergency calls. Boomers want what they want NOW! Dr. Jacobs said they call up on weekends and in the middle of the night, desperate to make appointments right away for some occasion the following week.

"Cosmetic surgery is becoming so common among some of these people," he says, "that they treat it like a trip to the hairdresser."

He also has a clinic in the Bahamas. "A woman can fly down on Wednesday, have her breast augmentation, recuperate and relax in the sun for a couple of days, and fly back on Sunday—a new woman."

Dr. Jacobs constantly answers the call for cleavage, noting that there is a trend to larger breasts in the human-design industry—although he says New York women tend to purchase somewhat smaller breasts than women in other parts of the country. Is there a smaller profit margin for him selling a diminutive pair in New York than there is for the guy selling a pair of bodacious gazoongas in Omaha? "No," he replies.

Some patients bring in pages torn from *Playboy* to show the doctor exactly what they have in mind. Or they bring in pictures of models with perfect noses. He is proud to say there is no single, readily identifiable "Jacobs Nose." In the neighborhood where he grew up, he says, it seemed like all teenaged girls had either the "Diamond Nose" or the "Goldman nose," named after the doctors who performed thousands of them, all variations of the scooped nose with the upturned tip.

His desk drawers are crammed with all sorts of silicone and inflatable implants, which he is delighted to pull out and demonstrate. "Look at this," he said, whipping out a silicone chin implant and sticking it on his chin. "It comes with a dimple too!" (No extra charge.)

In the waiting room, with its walls of mirrors, patients said they overhear the most fascinating discussions. There was the woman whose buttocks-lift (performed by another doctor) went askew, forcing her to stand for the last three months, even through dinner parties.

"I became ill when I tried on swimming suits," said one 48-year-old patient. She actually bought a swimsuit, wore it to the doctor's office, and told him to just "get rid of everything bad that shows."

"I came to see Dr. Jacobs for collagen shots," said Sharon, just 32 years old. "The man I'm trying to get to marry me is coming in from Paris. I kept buying new party dresses and taking them back. I had my hair done and that didn't work. I finally realized that these two little lines from my nose to my mouth were making me look drawn, tired and haggard. Having had them treated, people tell me I look happier now. One of my friends said I was vain to do this, but now I think that she is a very, very sloppy person."

"I'm going to Bali in February, and I couldn't go looking like I did," said Tanya, who had Dr. Jacobs liposuction her thighs, hips, and abdomen. She was in her mid-twenties!

Dr. Jacobs says people come in younger and younger for less and less reason. "They have maybe two little wrinkles," he says. "I tell them that a couple of wrinkles looks more natural than the ultratight, mannequin look, but they say that they don't care, they want them gone. They don't want to wait and undergo a radical change all at once."

"I had my eyes done for Thanksgiving," said Jean, another of his patients.

"I had mine done for my fortieth birthday," said Maura. "Dr. Jacobs suggested I might want to have my eyeliner tattooed on at the same time, but I passed on that one."

Men now make up as much as 20 percent of cosmetic surgery patients nationally. "Attitudes are changing," said George, a steel-company executive, who is pleased with his Dr. Jacobs nose job. "People in business see something like this as showing an overall aggressiveness and go-forwardness. The trend is to, you know, be all that you can be."

Lean and mean and youthful is what employers want, say many men and women coming in for surgery. One businessman suggested that he is competing for jobs now "with women who know all the tricks of looking younger with hairdos and makeup."

But Dr. Jacobs says more and more men are coming in saying they don't want surgery for professional reasons but just for themselves. "That tells me the stigma is gone," says Dr. Jacobs.

(Geraldo had his crow's-feet removed on live TV, presumably while continuing to discuss the O. J. verdicts.)

The doctor told of a strong, rugged man, "a contruction-worker type" with a dark beard and a muscular build who came in for a nose job. "I told him I'd give him a strong, masculine nose to match his face. And he told me that he cross-dresses on weekends and would prefer something more feminine."

"It's tough to maintain your status professionally or socially," said the 32-year-old Sharon. "There is always someone new, someone younger coming in and challenging you. You constantly have to sell and resell yourself."

One Upper East Side woman said that she has had all manner of cosmetic surgery work done, including a nose job and face-lift, but that lately her friends have told her that "maybe I am too good looking, or too conventional looking. I wouldn't mind a little character put back in my face. What do you think?"

I think wrinkles could become trendy, so for the time being, I'm hanging on to mine.

Health Clubbed

*I*have thought about exercise. Read about it. Watched it. Even considered it. Doctors recommend it, especially when they can't think of anything else to say.

When you're this age you go to the doctor and you're telling him that this hurts and that hurts and that you're tired all the time. You know the doctor just wants to blurt out: "What the hell do you expect? You're o-l-d. Old!" But they don't say that, because they like to have you keep coming in so they can just kind of look you over and charge you three hundred bucks.

At my last checkup—(1988?)—I was complaining about a multitude of maladies visiting my body. (Most have since moved in.) And the doctor looked bored—kind of listless, like he might need a checkup himself—and said rotely what he always says: "Are you getting enough exercise?" This is a diagnosis? He said it kind of like you or I might say: "Hot enough for ya?"

I replied that I did not exercise at all, which I considered just about the right amount.

I told him I could, I suppose, exercise . . . except . . . it's too cold out for that right now, and of course I have no time, I'm already late for work every day as it is, and I don't understand those newfangled exercise machines and I really can't get up that early, because I may well be sleep deprived. I mean, sure, there are maniacs out running in the predawn darkness getting hit by cars at 6 A.M. and nuts swimming at the Y, but . . .

He recommended I join a health club. Since he spent all those years in med school I thought I'd humor him. I started cutting out newspaper coupons for health clubs, which allowed you to join for, like, ninety-nine cents in springtime because all the fat people who joined up as a New Year's resolution have quit. That's my theory.

The clubs convenient to my house all have names like "Today's Woman." (My teenaged daughter goes there, and I'll bet the other women just hate it when she and her nonfat friends show up.) I guess some men do go there, but I could not. I had to quit going to my barber, even though he was great, because the place professed to be unisex, but in reality it was me in there with fifty women talking nail wraps and Sally Jessy Raphaël. We were all getting our hair "styled." Now I go to a guys-only place and we talk about the point spread on the Super Bowl and I get a hair "cut." It only costs half as much when they call it a "cut."

I visited a health club near work. "Welcome to the New York Health and Racquet Club," chirped a twenty-five-year-old Perfect Specimen. "I'm Pam!" I waited to hear the specials but instead she said: "I'm here to start you on the road to fitness." She really did.

I didn't want to dampen her enthusiasm—not that even a stroll through a car wash could—by telling her that I didn't really want to embark on that "road to fitness." That looong, hard road, with no rest areas. I wanted to hitch a ride on a streetcar named "Liposuction."

She demonstrated the Stairstepper at thirty-five strokes per minute. She showed me the treadmills and the Biodyne machine, and she spoke a different language, using words unfamiliar to me, like "quads" and "delts," "glutes," and "lats".

I kept envisioning Pam in black boots with a bullwhip. Or worse: my army drill instructor. I couldn't help noticing the striking similarities some of these big black exercise machines with gears and pulleys bore to medieval torture devices. There was a grunting, groaning man on one of them who wore a facial expression I'd seen somewhere before . . . it was the same face Mel Gibson wore in *Braveheart* when the king's henchmen had him on the rack.

The place was like a living S-M museum; a Williamsburg for torture freaks. Pam showed me the scary super pullover machine with all those gears and pulleys, and a chest press that reminded me of a restraining device on an electric chair. Didn't the Geneva Convention outlaw this kind of thing?

They say that doing all this prolongs your life; but I think your life just *seems* longer. And we do it voluntarily. And pay for the privilege. It's like Disney's Purgatory-Land: a lifetime of jogging, pedaling, and climbing stairs—to nowhere. Why, it's almost hamster-esque.

I asked this fit guy at work who always brings a gym bag to the office where he exercises, and he recommended I check out a fitness place called the Vertical Club.

It was a mistake to ask someone fit. As I waited in the Vertical Club for the prospective-member tour I admired a (too) attractive young woman in a leopard-striped leotard standing at the juice bar enjoying some lowfat yogurt. Along came a very handsome (*The Young and the Restless*–quality), sweaty stranger with really good deltoid definition, who sidled up to the bar and ordered carob peanuts and freshly squeezed grapefruit juice—the large. He turned slowly, looked her in the eyes, and spoke.

"Yogurt is mucous forming," he said coolly.

"My name is Sharon," she replied.

They repaired to their respective locker rooms for massive grooming projects and departed healthily into the night.

"We have no fat people here," said Tom, the manager.

"People join other health clubs to get in shape before they join here," explained a club supervisor.

Were they rejecting my application, warning me, or simply passing on a fascinating bit of information?

They showed me into the main exercise area, which was a vast, teeming, gleaming room of mirrored walls and wraparound neon, all aflutter with hundreds of exercise disciples and energizing rock music. "You might as well jump!" prodded a Van Halen recording, and the aerobics class did as it was told.

The club membership was grunting, discreetly, on more than 250 of the very latest chrome exercise machines (think of the usable energy they could be generating), machines kept glistening by a squad of cleaning personnel. Members jogged on a bouncy track that seemed almost to run for them. They furiously pedaled exercise bicycles, with digital calorie burn-rate readouts, on their way to where they were going. An already perfect specimen explained that she was pedaling wildly toward her goal of looking great in her swimming suit on Memorial Day in Southampton. Her odds (among other things) were good.

"The Vertical Club is today's Studio 54," said High Voltage, an actual person. Miss Voltage, aerobics instructor and personal trainer, was a bizarre hybrid of the show-business and physical-conditioning industries, with glitter in her hair and sequined leg warmers. This crackling little nerve ganglion of a woman had the disconcerting habit of doing stretching exercises during normal conversation and suddenly flying into the splits! You couldn't understand her but you certainly got the point.

An assistant manager sat calmly in the center of all this, cutting up little white slips of paper that the exercisers kept coming over and grabbing in their sweaty hands. They'd scribble down the name and telephone number of someone they'd just met who might be useful to them—socially or professionally or perhaps in providing the name of a good plumber.

"People see someone they like," the assistant manager said, "and they ask me things like the person's name, telephone number, job, marital status, sexual preference, whether they rent or own in the Hamptons, things like that. Two couples I introduced are married."

He said space at the makeup mirrors in the locker room was often strongly contested by women about to take the exercise floor. In addition to water-based makeup that doesn't run when perspiration occurs, "sport perfumes" and "sport jewelry" are also applied. A fifteen-hundred-dollar gold Cartier "tennis bracelet" was a current favorite. Reebok sport shoes and Ellesse sportswear—a sweat suit selling for $325—were also in vogue.

"It is better socially than a singles bar because it's not so obvious," said the supervisor. "You also don't meet as many lowlife creeps and insistent drunks. It's safer. The only problem here is that a lot of these people look like they'd rather go home and look at themselves than somebody else."

We said our good-byes, the Vertical Club supervisor and I, each knowing it was for the last time.

I Ab-stain

Whatever happened to those perfectly fine, old-fashioned weight-loss contraptions? The ones that looked like converted paint-can shakers, where all you had to do was strap a belt around your midsection, plug it into the wall socket, and stand there while the machine just jiggled the fat right off you into thin air? You didn't have to do a thing—although it was possible to mix your après-workout martinis while you exercised.

Today what have we got? We've got the Ab Roller, Ab Isolator, Abflex, Abworks, Pro Ab-Trainor, and the Ab Blaster Plus—just to name a few. Just to name the ones being advertised right now, all at this very moment, on my TV.

It's difficult not to succumb when there are six commercials on six separate channels for six different—but not all *that* different—semicircular, molded tubular abdominal exercise machines, each far, far better than the one on the next channel: one has a softer headrest, the next is easier to assemble, the one after that stores easily under your bed (not to be seen again until the garage sale).

The Abflex is different, this big plastic thing that looks like a toy Millennium Falcon spaceship that Hans Solo and Chewbacca piloted in *Star Wars,* except instead of playing with it, you press it against your abdomen—you know, sort of like if it were making a crash landing on that big bulbous Death Star Station?

Spandexed spokesmodels for these ab apparati look fantastic and promise that you will too, guaranteeing you'll lose ten pounds in ten days, four to six inches around the waist, and that, moreover, the device will "change your life!" Tony Little, famous hyperactive TV trainer (whose thyroid really ought to be milked twice daily) shrieks: "IF YOU DON'T HAVE AN AB-ISOLATOR YOU'RE, LIKE, WEIRD!" And yet . . . Tony himself . . . has one . . . so . . .

Magazine covers shout: "Best Abs Hips Butt Legs" (is that a complete sentence?); "Great Abs, No Sit-ups"; "Killer Abs." There are scads of new ab books, ab videos, special abs exercise classes, and a new fashion trend to short blouses that show off your midriff (not mine). The venerable QVC shopping network (official purveyor of official presidential inaugural souvenirs) reported selling a Wieder forty-dollar Ab-Shaper every second for fifteen hours.

The biggest seller has been the Ab Roller Plus, promising "a flat, sexy stomach in five minutes flat!" Doctors always spoil all the fun by telling us there's no such thing as "spot fat reduction"—that these ab machines won't do it alone, that you have to actually reduce caloric intake. But, we don't need no stinking evidence, thanks. We just keep on buying.

Just be aware that when a guy comes on an infomercial declaring "I got an Ab-Stractor 5000 and lost thirty pounds in thirty days!" there's probably something he's not telling you—

like shortly after purchasing the Ab-Stractor he was shot down behind enemy lines and has spent the past thirty days eating bugs and washing them down with perspiration from his socks.

Personally, I'm waiting for the Ab-Stainer. Not that I am not susceptible to infomercial items. I do own the Ginzu knives that will "Cut Tin Cans!" whenever that opportunity arises—and it will, it will. I also have the classic Popeil Pocket Fisherman that allows me to just pull off the road at any time, throw a line into any drainage ditch, and enjoy delicious panfish. Not to mention the miraculous, planet-friendly Popeil trash masher (in avocado) that operates energy free. Simply: 1. Put in trash 2. Put on lid 3. Sit on it.

However, I am not about to shell out money for something that will make me expend effort and possibly even perspire. Not when there are fine, equally effective products out there like the Elysee Body Toner, which promises in its magazine ads: "No Exercise. No Dieting. No Pills! You Quickly Shape Up—Doing Nothing at All." How? How do you think? "Advanced European Technology," dipshit. No workout togs appear necessary. This beautiful model in black-lace underwear is wearing the Body Toner belt around her waist that's delivering the miraculous electronic impulses that "duplicate the effect of a total workout so you get all the benefits . . . in just ten minutes a day while you watch TV, read a book, or take a relaxing break." (From what?!) Only $129.30, plus a free forty-dollar jar of thigh cream! I don't know about you, but we're always out of thigh cream at our house. (But, then, we do make a lot of beef stroganoff.)

The ad says "Now you can say goodbye to sit-ups, crunches, leg lifts, and all those expensive and bulky machines"—not knowing I never said "hello." I'm told that a lot of guys are buying those electric Craftmatic beds so they don't even have to sit up in order to get out of bed in the morning. (Another market segment is said to be guys buying the beds just to see if they can blow themselves.)

Under a commercial blitzkrieg for ab gadgets, it is only a certain toughness, an inner strength, a special something, an extraordinary gift, a sixth sense, the third rail . . . that keeps me from picking up that phone and ordering, that restrains me from physical exercise, that keeps me at one with the couch, watching these incessant (while informative) infomercials while devouring fistfuls of greasy chips. (I can eat a can of Pringles in five handfuls; my son in four—it's called evolution).

Sure, I could be thin and attractive too if I exercised, just like I could have been valedictorian (instead of Magna Non Laude)—if I'd studied. But I don't choose to play society's little games.

I enjoy sitting and watching the taut, spandexed spokes-models smiling as they roll up and back, effortlessly trimming and toning. And it is enough for me, as a Christian, to be happy for her without coveting her tautness.

Ab Worship *is* something of a religion now, and six-channel saturation coverage makes abdominal muscle development the predominate subject of mass communication in our society to-day. At this moment, the afternoon talk shows ("Dyslexic Lesbian Nuns' Psychic Diet Tips!") occupy only five channels; all-sports networks, a measly four; and O. J. panel discussions have somehow dropped off to just two! (Call your cable operator.)

When television was invented, communications experts proclaimed that this modern miracle medium would elevate, educate, and just plain better all mankind. Everyone assumed the experts meant that TV would elevate mankind *intellectually*—and that the experts had been terribly, terribly wrong (e.g., *Baywatch, Jenny Jones* et al., ad nauseam).

But it turns out that what the experts must have meant is that television would benefit mankind *abdominally*! Having "killer abs," "washboard abs"—perhaps a veritable "six-pack" of tight, rippling muscles—has become perhaps the best quality Today's Citizen can possess. (Commercials for encyclopedias currently occupy no channels, as the brain becomes more and more like the appendix, another useless organ.)

This is not good news for the likes of me. I am moving away from washboard abs and closer to wash *tub* abs. Away from six-packs, more toward the keg look. This is a physical trend that is ongoing throughout the forties and becomes accompanied by an attitudinal change at fifty that is at odds with reversing that physical trend. (Let's call that attitudinal change "Not Really Giving a Damn," shall we?)

It sounds like just another bad attitude, but I have come up with a cheap philosophical foundation for my (supine) position. A few enlightened souls, like Stephen Levine, a meditation teacher and author who conducts mind-body workshops around the country, sees abs this way: "This fixation on stomach muscles is a bad thing. We have to get to a deeper level of self-image, something more meaningful than good abs. When you harden your belly you are withdrawing from the people around you. The most grief, fear, and distrust is held in the hard belly. It is a resistance to life. The hard belly is a violent belly."

Think Buddha. And pass the Bavarian creme-filleds. No. The box.

Treadmills & Other Torture Devices

*B*efore Ab Rollers, Thigh-masters ruled the airwaves. I didn't buy one of those either, although I always enjoyed watching Suzanne Somers demonstrate them. She and I took her thighs seriously.

Before that, there was the StairMaster, which I also did not purchase since I live in an older home that already has three flights of stairs, so why would I go out and buy more?

And before that, I did not buy an expensive step-aerobics box—a fifty-dollar box!

Nor did I buy a rowing machine, although there is frequently plenty of navigable water in my basement.

Nor an exercycle, because the ones with those cool computer scenes to ride through cost, like, three thousand dollars!

I didn't buy one of those multipurpose gyms with gears and pulleys either.

And I passed on the NordicTrack, because I can't ski, and if I could it would be in a beautiful place with the beautiful people, not down there next to my water heater.

I know people who have *all* this stuff, with all manner of electronic gauges and beepers that tell you when you're dead and the like. One friend has a treadmill—the Trotter 540 Super Trainer—in his office. Personally I've been thinking about a hammock. He says exercise gets your blood flowing, heart pumping, metabolism jumping. He says it gives him more energy, but the few times I've exercised in the morning I've always had to lie down in the afternoon. On my office floor. Diagonally. Small office. And I have to time it just right. If cleaning personnel were to unlock the door to empty my wastebasket, they'd knock me out cold.

It's not like I missed my chance with all these exercise contraptions, they're all just so much garage-sale fodder and readily available any weekend.

What I do own is a Jane Fonda aerobic workout tape, still sealed in the original cellophane. I don't actually do aerobics, but I do watch sometimes—not so much your Richard Simmons as those girls on the beach. Yes, as a matter of fact they do wear bikinis, but it's not about that. It's about cardiovascular fitness.

And we do own a treadmill. But I didn't buy that either. It belonged to a friend of ours, a man in his early fifties who used it almost every day. His widow gave it to us.

I use it on occasion. Most of the time I can't because I get up too late, and besides, the treadmill is in the basement next to the washing machine and is often already in use as a clothesline for drying sweaters and such. Informal surveys I've conducted among friends suggest that this is the kind of thing most home exercise equipment is used for. Two billion dollars' worth of expensive, computerized clothes hangers a year! One woman we know uses the timer on her Biocycle for baking cookies. Thirty-five hundred dollars. Who says you can't put a price on health? They not only put a price on it, they mark it up. The price tags are enough to give you cardiac arrest.

Next to our treadmill is a weight-lifting bench with a set of free weights that belong to my son, who quit using them after high school football. The bench is used exclusively as a laundry way station now. I used to actually lift the weights from time to time, but it was too much trouble taking off almost all the weights (the bar is even heavy) to make it light enough for me to use, then putting them all back on so as not to let people know what a weenie I really am.

My wife frequently uses our treadmill. She cranks it up to four MPH, sets it at a 2 percent incline, listens to the Temptations on her earphones, sings along too loudly (and flatly), pumps hand weights—and keeps it all up for at least half an hour. My son and my daughter actually *run* on the thing, which seems overly rigorous to me and somewhat dangerous. They're both tall and they bounce up and down when they run and come upstairs with acoustical tile deposits in their hair.

I don't run on the treadmill and I don't often use the little hand weights either, although I do hold the remote TV clicker, which is about the same number of ounces as the little hand weights I use. (I switch the remote from one hand to the other so one arm doesn't become overdeveloped.)

I hate getting up a half hour early to walk on the treadmill. So sometimes I just walk for ten minutes. At this age I hate getting up at all, frankly, for any reason. I roll out and immediately put on my exercise outfit that I keep next to the bed. Calvin Klein Sport it is not: green bermuda shorts; the T-shirt I wear as pajamas; semi-clean sweat socks; and my Nikes, circa 1988. I bought them at the Seoul Olympics, spending thousands of dollars to get there and getting five bucks off on the shoes at the Nike tent.

I fire up the treadmill. Enter my weight: 190—not bad at all for someone my height: seven six. Enter the speed: 2.5 MPH—to warm up. Set the incline: 0.0—almost steep for someone who grew up on the flatlands of Illinois and whose driveway was the steepest slope for miles around. I don't do hills: jogging, cycling, and especially skiing. When I walk someplace that is noticeably downhill I always try to arrange for return transportation.

And we're off! At 2.5 MPH, which would be "Baby Crawl" if speeds had names like they do ("Liquefy") on the blender. I think of 2.5 as "Energy Saver"—I'm very ecologically minded.

I warm up and cool down at 2.5 and try to keep the time in between at a minimum. I increase the speed to 2.8, then 3.0 for a few seconds, and on to 3.2 and 3.5, before leaping to hyperspace: 4.0.

At 4.0 I have to hold on to the front railing or I start losing ground. My shoulder blades begin to knock down the wall hangings and my heels start punching holes in the drywall; 4.5 is out of the question. I hold the railing as I would the rear bumper of a speeding car.

Except at high speeds, where I risk an accident, treadmills are dreadfully tedious and TV becomes an essential diversion. You have to have the remote control in hand because you might turn on Regis interviewing somebody interesting only to have Kathy Lee jump in and start talking about Cody before you can risk life and limb by jumping off, changing channels, and re-mounting the moving treadmill like some latter-day John Wayne stopping a runaway stagecoach team.

I don't like the treadmill, but I guess when you walk for fifteen minutes at three MPH the endorphins don't really get a chance to kick in.

When I was growing up, lab rats were the only things that ran on treadmills—usually with little rat cigarettes dangling from their ratty little lips. No normal person would have set foot on a treadmill, not voluntarily, not back then, in the Age of Reason.

People in those days came home from work quite tired enough, thanks. My mom and dad liked to sit down when they had the chance. Now Sears—catering to the salt of the earth—sells a quarter million treadmills a year.

Back then if you had extra energy at the end of the day you'd have to put it to good use doing chores, not walking to nowhere just to burn it off.

Now, they do say you can use your time on the treadmill productively, by listening to French 101 tapes, reading magazines, watching PBS, or making business calls on a cell phone. (Personally, I prefer *Dukes of Hazzard* reruns.)

Or making grilled cheese sandwiches. At 2.5 I can safely use the adjacent toaster oven to make them. The treadmill tells me I'm burning calories while I walk, but it doesn't know about the grilled cheese sandwiches.

Golf &
Other Old
Sports

*A*t fifty, one plays golf. I'd still play basketball if you could use carts.
When you're young you play baseball and basketball and other games where the ball moves. When you're fifty you either play doubles tennis, where *you* don't move, or golf, where the ball doesn't. Or you watch others play these games on TV.

I predict sumo wrestling will become the next big sport for boomers, because it actually *requires* participants to be fat and it only lasts three seconds. Right now, of course, golf and fishing are the ones really taking off—sports that involve cocktails. Millions of boomers are taking up golf, hundreds of new courses open every year. A man I know built a five-million-dollar business paying frogmen to dive into water hazards and retrieve golf balls that he would then resell. He retired at about my age.

Most of my friends play, but I choose not to inflict my own peculiar style of play (bad) upon them. They say they don't mind lousy players, but I don't think they've really seen such depths of lousiness.

They tell me that playing golf is good for business, but with me it would probably be the medical business, the personal-injury business, the window-replacement business.

I play once or twice a year, on vacation, usually with my son, who is likewise not good. We play on public courses using rental clubs. The bags are ripped, the drivers have screws protruding from the bottoms, and the balls are used and abused. That is, the equipment is a pretty good match for our level of play.

We buy the thirty-six ball Family Pak for a nine-hole course. No sense buying too many, we can always come back. He and I played in Vermont once without enough balls and when I hit someone's house—Thwack!—I had to sneak up onto the front porch to get our last ball.

There was a sign on the little clubhouse where we played on a recent vacation reading "NO NUISANCE GOLFERS," and we glanced at each other. Should we leave? No, it's not like we're nuisances on purpose. Little that we do on the golf course is on purpose.

We sat down and waited for the first tee to clear. We didn't want anyone around when we teed off. In front or back. We don't like people watching. It doesn't hurt our game, it hurts our feelings. Sometimes the guy in the clubhouse will insist on making a foursome, pairing us up with two real golfers and ruining our whole day—not to mention theirs. Yes, it takes pretty much the whole day for us to play nine holes.

That day it helped that the guy ahead of us drove off the first tee and sliced his shot onto the adjacent green for the ninth hole—nearly a hole in one! Public courses are that way. Guys playing in blue-jeans cutoffs and mesh T-shirts who swing at golf balls like they're blindfolded and trying to bust a piñata.

I was nervous. I hit a tee shot *behind* me once. It is possible:

straight up with heavy backspin. To compensate, I top this ball and send it bounding through the right rough. My tall and powerful son hits his drive a long, long way . . . somewhere.

We spend a lot of time looking for balls (no machete in the golf bag?) and we spend a lot of time teeing off. When there's no one around we may tee off three or four times until we hit one that's acceptable or until some groundskeeper yells: "Hey, this isn't a driving range."

I have actually played in a tournament, a national tournament: the Bad Golfers Association tournament, in Kansas City.

One hundred thirty-two truly terrible golfers from near and far gathered to test their ineptitude against other incompetents. You have to play against the worst to find out how bad you really are.

"There's twenty-five million golfers out there," said John McMeel, BGA president, "and only ten percent can break one hundred, so that gives us a great crowd to work with. There's more of us than them."

I played in a foursome with McMeel, Pat Oliphant, and John O'Day, who wasn't as bad as he should have been. But John and Pat were certainly qualified. President McMeel leads by example, consistently and earnestly playing really bad golf. Horrifying at times. Likewise Oliphant, the titular vice president.

Unfortunately, with this array of talent, not everyone could lose. Some set personal goals for themselves.

"I hope to do worse than anyone," said a fellow named Becker from Seattle. "I should be in the RBGA, the Really Bad Golfers Association. I think I shoot anywhere from one hundred to one-fifty, but I'm not sure I ever kept score."

But it's not enough to talk a bad game, you've got to go out there and prove yourself on the field of play. And that they did. The games began, and so did balls smacking into trees and splashing down in water hazards. Sand and sod were flying— along with a few clubs—and dozens of golfers could be seen wandering through trees and brush looking for lost balls. Oh, you'd see some golfers on the fairways, of course, but not always the fairway corresponding to the hole they were playing. It wasn't pretty.

Galleries were smaller than those you see on the PGA tour. Two onlookers sat on a bench well off a fairway and confided that sometimes they got *behind* the bench.

With scores soaring, these golfers started taking things into their own hands. Oliphant demonstrated a perfect way to blast out of a sand trap, simulating a golf shot by throwing sand into the air and tossing the golf ball up on the green in one motion. A beautiful thing to watch when done properly. Oliphant could also pick up his ball on the fairway from a moving golf cart and toss it onto the green with great accuracy. Very impressive, but you have to remember that he's been cheating a long, long time. These guys use their feet adroitly, too, kicking balls out of the rough soccer-style—all of this in full accordance with BGA rules.

"Our creed, credo, or whatever," said Oliphant, "is that if you can get away with it you can do anything."

McMeel explained, "We don't like to call it cheating, Bill, it's just like if a ball has an 'awkward' lie, you can 'adjust' it with feet or hands—anything as long as you're not seen."

On the other hand the rules are quite strict in certain areas.

"Acts contrary to the definition of BGA status," McMeel explained, "would include receiving the help of a golf professional. So if you take a lesson . . . you're out."

"If you get caught," Oliphant added.

How do they really feel about being chronically bad golfers?

"It hurts sometimes," McMeel acknowledged. "I've noticed that every time I'm invited out it's always once. No repeats, no returns. I was invited to Augusta, where they play the Masters, and at the end of the third day my host said 'John, take a look around because you ain't going to see this place again.' And he meant it."

Who out of all these bad golfers would be Worst-of-Field? It wouldn't be easy to tell. Some golfers filled out their score-cards before they took the course because that's how they always do it. But I noted that most of the players didn't seem to be writing anything down.

"Would you?" snapped McMeel.

Not to worry, in the BGA Open, everyone's a loser. And that's the beautiful thing.

There used to be public courses in New York City that matched my game.

I saw a man, Don Jerome, hit into an abandoned car on a course in the Bronx.

What's the penalty for hitting into an abandoned car? "I'm not sure there's been a PGA ruling on that," answered Kimble Knowlden, a man who had been hired to upgrade the city's courses by solving problems, from waist-high weeds to muggers.

He was out talking to golfers, and did he ever get an earful. Mr. Jerome said that a friend of his was robbed of sixty-five dollars and his credit cards while lining up a chip shot. Mr. Jerome noted that something like this can disrupt a golfer's concentration.

"We are in a mild state of shock hearing all this," said Knowlden, who worked for the American Golf Corporation, of

Los Angeles, and who was once a golf pro at Pebble Beach, one of the world's grandest courses.

"I know a guy," said city golfer James McDonald, "who used to take his guard dog with him to the golf course, and another guy carried Mace in his golf bag."

Charlie Pessoni told Knowlden that instead of twosomes and foursomes, sometimes he and his friends would play in eightsomes for protection.

"I was never bothered," commented James Murphy.

"You carried a gun," Mr. Pessoni replied.

"There were assaults and robberies right on the courses!" said Knowlden, more accustomed to dealing with problems like divots and tee times. "There was graffiti all over everything. The well water in Staten Island was so polluted that when we watered the grass it turned black."

"Tell him about the bodies, Kimble," said John DeMatteo, one of Knowlden's colleagues. "We get a certain number of dead bodies. I try not to be the first one out on the course in the morning."

Sportsitting

*E*ndorphins don't hold a candle to fettuccine Alfredo.

I never got a "runner's high." I ran in high school on the cross-country team and hated it. Ever try to pick up chicks wearing a cross-country letter? Impossible.

At fifty, few of us are runners anymore. Most have succumbed to bad knees, mean dogs, heart attacks, or cars. I walk some, but am more into sitting down these days. On the day before the New York Marathon, I stopped into a recliner-chair store to be with my own kind.

"Marathon runners are crazy," said Ralph Sansone, fifty-one, who had come to the La-Z-Boy Showcase Shoppe in Flushing, Queens, to look for yet a third recliner chair for the den.

"They say jogging is healthy and relieves stress—well, this is how I do it," he said pulling back the lever that flipped up the foot rest, then tilting back, all the way back to a position suitable for root-canal work—and closing his eyes.

When 18,365 runners take off across the Verrazano-Narrows Bridge the next day, Mr. Sansone will be at one with his favorite cocoa-colored—or is that the mocha?—Naugahyde recliner, watching it on television. Me too.

Not all of it. Even *watching* runners for prolonged periods makes people like Ralph and me weary, so we'll hit our remote-control switches soon after the dramatic start of the race to watch pro football. He says that from time to time he will reach down into a small polystyrene cooler to the left of his chair for a can of cold beer, and to his right, where pretzels will be positioned. The man has personal comfort down to a science.

"I honestly don't think running would be good for Ralph," notes Mrs. Sansone. "People die running, and dogs bite them."

Another customer at the shop, Rita Hastings, commented that sometimes she has problems extricating her husband from his recliner at mealtime and bedtime. Indeed La-Z-Boy has manufactured models with food trays attached as well as with side pockets for copies of *TV Guide*.

"When I get the urge to jog," says Bernie Berger, a salesman, "I climb into one of these chairs until it passes. We had one of the marathon runners in here looking at the chairs the other day. He needs one. Running makes him awfully tired."

"All these exercise books," Mr. Berger continued, "do more harm than good. There is no supervision and people hurt themselves. Orthopedics has become the greatest business in the world. Instead of all this running around, people should sit down."

A lot of them have. Employees and customers at the store cited tendinitis, shinsplints, heel spurs, knee surgery, tedium, and their inability to get out of bed early enough to jog before work as reasons they gave up on physical fitness.

Such injuries and unpleasantries are rare in sport sitting. One sitter noted that expensive, special equipment and outfits are not required for this popular form of inactivity.

Although most sitters believe that runners are addicts and that they never smile until they stop, the sitters acknowledge that running is no doubt beneficial to cardiovascular and over-all fitness. But Mr. Sansone pointed out that although running may reduce the heart rate, sometimes it reduces the rate to zero, a dangerous level. Also he said that a man in his neighborhood had been hit by a car while running and that another is on crutches with a severely sprained ankle.

"Our chairs aid circulation," contended Stan Lozinski, the store manager, as he sat down and threw the lever that dropped him into the supine position. "See, my feet are higher than my head now." This, of course, could improve blood flow to the brain, allowing the sitter to make better TV-viewing decisions, helping PBS, hurting Geraldo.

"The chairs support your back," Mr. Lozinski continued to contend, "doctors recommend them." He didn't mention any names.

Lillian Fontane, store employee, is one who can attest to the chairs' ability to reduce heart and breathing rates, having fallen asleep in one the day before on the showroom floor—an occupational hazard at the Shoppe.

Joe Hastings came in to close the deal on a new $435 orange and gold Herculon tweed recliner with "Early American" de-sign overtones. (George Washington could have used one of these after a tough day with the redcoats.) Joe bore witness to the chairs' health benefits: "When I sit in my old one at home with a highball there is no need whatsoever for my blood pres-sure pills." (Consult your cardiologist.)

He said as wonderful as it is, however, "you do have to take breaks from the sitting."

For all the differences between runners and sitters there are similarities. Mr. Sansone practices the runner's habit of "carbo loading." As he sits watching TV he often eats spaghetti and drinks beer—something runners do to replace fluids and potassium in their bodies. Just how much potassium is lost during, say, *MacGyver* reruns, has never been accurately measured.

He admits that sitting doesn't burn as many calories per hour as running, and he has switched recently to light beer. He has so far, however, been unable to cut down his consumption of nacho cheese, but how else, one wonders, to provide the nacho every human body needs?

An athlete in high school, Ralph still remains so inclined, watching as many as six televised games each week, and he sometimes even watches aerobics classes.

"Our customers are your traditional-type people," says Mr. Lozinski, not the kind to lie around in a sensory-deprivation tank or run marathons to relieve stress.

"You can buy a chair," he said, "for the price of a couple pairs of those fancy running shoes. I'll take a recliner and a good movie on the VCR anytime."

"Admittedly," said Mrs. Fontane, who has given up her walking exercise routine, "there isn't the feeling of accomplishment in sitting. And sitting doesn't make you feel invigorated."

Yet Mrs. Sansone alluded to her husband's achieving something that sounded similar to a Zen-like state when he nestles in front of the television in his recliner, a blanket over his legs, a Jets game on, the remote in one hand, and a beer in the other.

No euphoria-producing beta-endorphins are released as happens while running, but Mr. Sansone testifies to regularly achieving a "sitter's high."

Walk
Don't Run

Right next to the new reading glasses store at the local mall is a new "walking store"—it sells walking shoes, apparel, and accessories.

Leave it to the American entrepreneur of the nineties to turn walking into a trendy new business after four million years of bipedalism.

Too old to run, baby boomers have dialed down their treadmills to Walk. Actually, mine's set on Meander. I walk on my treadmill and even outdoors sometimes. I'll walk four blocks to Baskin-Robbins (and back, wiseass). Our friends, the Walkers, exercise walk (downhill) to our house for a beer, and we drive them home.

Sometimes we walk at the recreation field, but the slippery green goose crap is awfully deep. (A little napalm and it's Christmas dinner for everybody!) Sometimes we walk on the high school track, but there I have to break into a run whenever I see my son's football coach so he won't think I'm a wuss. Sometimes we even walk on the prescribed county walking track, where earnest walkers wearing Walkmans march along the track, oblivious to the surrounding woods, the adjacent stream, the waterfowl, everything. A few are eating. Some are positively mummified in spandex as they stroll at 1.6 MPH— in *helmets*. Dear God, don't let them be *walking helmets*.

They look stupid, yes, but well turned out—better equipped for strolling than many Olympic athletes are for the marathon. Truly. And who was I to judge? Me, dressed not to walk, but to what? Mow the lawn? Sweatshirt, jeans, and, dare I admit it? Walking in running shoes!

I visited a walking store called The Urban Hiker, where one customer was lacing up some new walking shoes and asking another, "How long have you been walking?" To which came the reply, "Oh, about a month."

It sounded so strange. I mean if they had been toddlers shooting the breeze at a day-care center, fine, but these guys were "middle-aged."

The store carries everything you really don't need at all to walk around the block, such as two-hundred-dollar walking outfits and all manner of walking accessories, including imported, telescoping walking poles made of ultralight steel. And of course a myriad of "walking shoes." But . . . aren't . . . *all* . . . shoes . . . walking shoes?

A man came in and asked if the store carried "walking underpants." And, yes, it did. He said he already had the Pro-Walker walking shoes, a walking shirt, walking shorts, walking sweatsuit, and walking *socks*. Rockport walking socks. There are walking hats and walking gloves, too, perhaps for when you have to look up a lot of numbers in the Yellow Pages.

And how does all of this walking paraphernalia differ from, say, jogging outfits?

"In subtle ways," said George, the store owner. "Walking suits have maybe a little more style to them because, like, you might want to go in someplace." Like stores and restaurants.

Unlike, say, the hundred-yard dash or basketball or most other sports, shopping and eating can be done during sport walking.

"Walking is not something difficult," said George, and I wrote that one down. "So you can talk while you walk. It's nice."

George said walking can burn calories (albeit not very many) and relieve stress. George said one of the store's customers was George Balboa, who billed himself as "The Walking Psychotherapist," offering therapy that combines race walking and the Brazilian samba.

The store sold walking books, like the one entitled *The Walking Book*, with chapter titles like "Meet Your Feet" and instructions on how to walk: "Step 2: Defying gravity, we lean forward to overcome inertia." Very helpful. Except beginners in this sport usually can't read yet.

There were walking periodicals, like *Walking* magazine, with articles on how to walk, and ads for a walking video and a book entitled *Walk, Don't Die*, which "shows you how jogging kills, calisthenics cripple, diets debilitate, and aerobics disable." I agree.

George said his father thought he was nuts to open a walking store and told him: "Everybody walks! Why do you need a store to take a walk?"

What next? *Standing* magazine? A store called The Urban Napper, catering to sport nappers?

How old do baby boomers get before unassisted *breathing* is considered a form of exercise and Nike sells breathing suits and the $135 breathing shoes? ("And when you stop breathing they have our patented removable soles," chirps the salesman.)

Geezer Goods

*I*n search of a miracle cure for tennis elbow, I happen into an entire *store* full of products for the fifty-plus set.

A *Superstore!* A kind of Home Depot, a veritable Toys "R" Us for the geezerly, a store named "Take Good Care."

Twenty thousand square feet of—yes!—tennis-elbow remedies, reading glasses, large-type dictionaries, canes (now called walking sticks), pillboxes with built-in reminder beepers, antistress bath beads, industrial strength makeup, and sexual impotence machines (manual and electric hard drive)—in addition to serious business like twenty-four-hour emergency oxygen service, wheelchairs, and Medicare and Medicaid claims processing.

Trust the American entrepreneur to always be on top of things, one step ahead of the market, ready to ride the age wave.

"Excuse me, where are the glasses?" asks a sixtyish man at the front desk, which is kind of funny since they are right in front of him but he can't see them. "The optical department is center main aisle, straight ahead," says the receptionist.

Reading glasses are big here. Lots of stuff is big. Next to the glasses are large-type dictionaries and atlases, clocks with

Big Ben–sized numbers and clock radios giving the time in huge, Vegas-bright digits.

Joyce Greenberg, Take Good Care's creator, shows me the big-digit bathroom scales, but I'm quite happy with the one I already have, thanks, the one with numbers so small I can't possibly see them.

She shows me wristwatches that you don't have to see at all because they literally tell time—talking watches. There are Touch-Tone phones with numbers so big you could punch them with your fist, and newspaper viewing machines that magnify newsprint twenty times its original size. There are discreet little foldaway magnifying glasses for scrutinizing menus, and really big, indiscreet magnifiers you attach to your TV screen.

One fifty-something shopper says he loves this line of big items because, frankly, he can no longer see "jack shit."

I bypass the exercise department, filled with Ab-Rockits and hand weights and muscle resistance machines. Too strenuous. Instead, I try out the heating pads (ooh), the massagers (ooooh), and those seat lift chairs that hurl you across the room. I always thought these were for the terribly infirm, but now I wish taxis had them.

The miracle cure for my tennis elbow is called Tectonic Magnets. You strap magnets to your tennis elbow or your jogger's knees or your sinuses (that's attractive) or whatever hurts and the magnets "send forth a negative (unipole) field that counteracts the positive fields associated with pain." Really?

In the clothing department, here now, for the blue-jeans generation that's getting on in age, they have blue jeans and blue-jeans shirts with Velcro closures. And elastic shoelaces that allow you to slip on your shoes without retying them. Yes, they have them for running shoes.

Joyce shows me the electric beds. They come with dual controls, and for an extra five hundred dollars they'll vibrate. For the water-bed generation, there are water *pillows* that get rid of that crick in your neck. And anti-snore pillows, too.

And for this aging naturally (if ungracefully) generation: pillows stuffed with buckwheat hulls. Sure. And bottled aroma-therapy cures labeled "anti-stress" and "sensual harmony."

There's a media department with "anti-stress" CDs of sounds from the rain forest and tapes entitled "Forty-some-thing Forever," and a Zsa Zsa Gabor workout video. Really. "Maybe she hits people for exercise," was Joyce's guess.

There's a complete line of walkers and what Joyce called "rollators"—trendy new walkers with wheels.

"They come in sexy colors," she says, sounding a bit like a car salesman, "with padded seats, baskets, and hand brakes." I liked the Nova Cruiser Deluxe in teal. Drives the girls at the home absolutely nuts.

The next step is snazzy battery-powered scooters. The 1997 Pride Legend model seemed to have everything and ran twenty-three hundred dollars. But the saleswoman said I should wait (a good thirty years I hope) for the all-new Pride "Jazzy" model that was coming soon. A Jazzy brochure promises "high per-formance with elegant style . . . four brilliant colors . . . stylish MAG wheels . . . independent drive wheel suspension . . . cup holder . . . head and taillights and turn signals." Who wouldn't wait?

Are these things becoming status symbols? How long till BMW and Mercedes jump into the scooter market? How long until the seniors start souping them up and we see old codgers racing them on ESPN2?

We stroll through "Incontinence" to the "Games" section, where . . . what's her name? . . . showed me games to help with my short-term memory loss.

"Anything for libido problems?" I asked. "A friend wanted me to ask."

She shows me the Osbon Plus pump for men. Manual and electric. (Should I wait for the turbo?) I was trying to picture the manual and I had this vision of an old fella lying on his back with his favorite gal standing next to the bed pumping a bicycle pump. You definitely want to go electric, I thought, although Joyce said the electric is not covered by Medicare. Hillary was right: the health-care system does need reform.

A man probably in his late seventies came in and bought one, Joyce said, and when he left he told them: "I'll be in with my wife to buy another one tomorrow and you act like you never saw me before, OK?"

Boomers are turning 50 and the American entrepreneur is ready. Americans over 50 already account for 77 percent of the country's net worth and 41 percent of the consumer demand—and counting.

50's nifty now that we can get a discount at Lube Pro and free checking at Southern Trust. We've got Centrum Silver, Just For Men, Vanna White's new teeth whitening system, artificial hips, Revlon's Age Defying Makeup, liposuction, alphahydroxy skin technology, six different heartburn medicines advertising on the *CBS Evening News* alone, the Prime Life cable channel, large print *New York Times,* ginseng, testosterone patches, Oil of Olay, relaxed fit jeans, Depends, Sustacal and Ensure. "Will you come to my wedding, Grandpa?" asks the little girl in the commercial. If he drinks Ensure he will, princess, otherwise Grandpa will be dead!

Hell, free magazines arrive in the mail for us, unsolicited. I received one just today called *Lifetime—Knowledge for Adult Living.* Why do these adult living publications always have names like "Lifetime"? I guess focus groups suggest they shy away from "Deathtime" or "Sickly Time." On the cover is this fit-looking couple smiling as they walk vigorously in their jogging outfits. He has gray hair but otherwise looks 30. She has on a pink outfit with matching handweight dumbbells. The caption reads "Walk This Way—be stronger, ward off hypertension and osteoporosis; clear your head and revel in self-confidence. Sleep better." All right, we will.

Lifetime contains "Good News from Government" on the Older Americans Act. The ads invite me to "join the Fun at Bald Eagle Commons, North Jersey's 1st Active Adult Campus Community." Why, I can seem myself now, weaving one of those fruit baskets at the Creative Center! Or having fun at one of the Planned Events! Or enjoying shuffleboard/boccie.

There are ads for the Franciscan Oaks Lifecare Community, where they have skilled nursing care (could you get a price break by using unskilled?); for the Allendale Community for Mature Living, offering independent living, intermediate care, skilled medical care, and the meat wagon; for Lake Ridge, "the Active Adult Community," showing three women in a swimming pool each holding one arm over her head, four men playing boccie ball, a guy playing pool with his wife (!), and a guardhouse with gates just like at the minimum-security prisons. Nifty, I tell you.

You need not leave the safety and comfort of your own home to purchase geezer goods.

In addition to AARP applications, brochures for cemeteries, and invitations to estate planning seminars, at 50 you will also begin receiving catalogues with all manner of geezer-ware.

My favorite is *Dr. Leonard's Health Care* catalogue, and one of my favorite products in it is the new SuperKegel, which looks like some sort of medieval penis-trap that women hold between their legs. Called "the intimate exerciser" it is said to help you perform Kegel muscle exercises to "alleviate symptoms of incontinence, improve bladder control, and enhance sexual pleasure." You wondered what would follow ab machines and Thighmasters? Incontinence solvers. Watch for the infomercials as boomers age.

Another favorite in the new catalogue is the car seat swivel, a kind of lazy Susan that people my age can sit on for "easy in-easy out" action.

There is the device to "Loosen Tight Collars and Waistbands:—a waistband and collar extender for the increasingly fat. "Gives you breathing room—adding an inch to the waistband and a size to collars."

I really need that. And I really need the Handy Footrest, a plastic thing you rest your foot on when putting on socks and shoes. You slip it between your mattress and box spring. Right now I sit on edge of the bed and pull out a dresser drawer to rest my foot on so I don't have to bend over so far. "Good for trimming toenails too!"

I may be wrong but I think I spill more food on my shirts and ties and pants than I used to. No more! Not with the "attractive" neck-to-lap full-coverage mealtime protector made of wipe-clean waterproof vinyl. It looks like one of those shields you wear to have an X ray.

"Eliminate prune lips" reads another item. I had never heard this phrase before. Prune lips refers to age lines around the mouth area, which are apparently completely curable thanks to "Lips So Smooth" wrinkle cream.

There are La-Z-Boy recliner covers, denture repair kits, really ugly housedresses like your grandmother used to wear, toe separators, personal massagers the exact size and shape of a penis but which the dumb models are always using on their *shoulders*, trimming belts, tummy uplifters, butt enhancers, nitroglycerin pill holders, minoxidil, jumbo easy-to-see dominos, spring-loaded seat cushions that help you up, and pill splitters for half doses.

There are miracle cures and homeopathic remedies—"homeopathic" being the medical term for "doesn't really do anything."

Among these popular items offered by the good doctor Leonard are: coenzyme Q10, Siberian ginseng, chromium picolinate, Echinacea, hydroxycitric acid, mutton tallow, primrose oil, zinc lozenges, and fat absorber pills ("works like a sponge"), Great Sex Capsules and Cat's Claw Capsules that— stop the presses—cure *everything*. Everything.

Think that's a miracle? Listen to this. "Despondency" brand tablets are for the "safe, effective relief of anxiety, mood swings, the 'Blues,' emotional burnout, suppressed grief, and mental exhaustion." $12.99 for 250 tablets. Amazing.

There are your placenta creams, cow udder balms, and your "Face Lift In A Jar."

And Rejoyn, a hard rubber sheath you can stuff your soft penis in to "enjoy" sex, as well as a wide range of incontinence products like the sheath urinal and drainage bag, and the waterproof bed pad that goes conveniently on top of the sheets.

The good doctor is also offering a Will Kit. "Prepare your own legally valid will—No need for high-priced lawyers!" $6.99.

Actually, I want a living will. One that reads "Should I Ever Require Three or More Items from the *Doctor Leonard's Catalogue*—Please, Shoot Me. Thank you."

The Vision Thing

*J*ust as C.R.S. is setting in, you're hit with C.S.S. (Can't See Squat).

Lenscrafters calls us "emerging presbyopes." Such fast-glasses franchises sprout like Starbucks stores. Near me, Vision Express lures aging motorists off the highway by offering cheap, fast eyewear, "under $100" and "ready in just one hour."

Close. Mine were $475 and were ready in just three weeks. And I have to take them off to read. Admittedly, under the "Two-for-One" offer I did receive a "free" second pair for just $175.

Your eyes are the first, but certainly not the last, of the major organs to go. It can actually be a blessing at times. You look in the mirror and think you don't look too bad—when you most certainly do! You mistakenly spray Black Flag ant killer on your hair (sorry, honey), brush your teeth with tile and tub caulk, and stop sweeping the kitchen floor because, hey, it doesn't look dirty to you. And is your floor *really* dirty if you don't see it that way? It gets deep, the philosophy and the mess on the floor.

*   *   *

A group of fifty-year-olds out for dinner becomes a spectacle—no pun intended.

You can't read the menu. You can't hear the specials. And you couldn't remember them even if you could.

"I can't read this menu without my glasses," Barbara complains.

"It's upside down," Joe explains.

"Did the waiter say 'string beanies'?" Valerie asks.

"No, 'linguine,' " Artie replies.

"What was that third dish he mentioned?" asks Joyce, and her seven dining companions respond with blank stares, like so many *Jeopardy!* contestants with no points on the board.

It's a trendy menu we have before us this evening. The entrées are in rather small black type on a dark blue background. Hip, yes, but no one can read them. It's like a group eye examination, and all eight of us are failing.

People are holding the menus up for more light, squinting to read them, and comparing notes.

Vince: "Does that, right there, really say 'Happy Meal'?"

Joyce: "I think it's 'Snappy Veal'—maybe a Cajun dish?"

Jody: "It might say 'Happy Veal.' Is this Chinese food?"

As for the translation of ratatouille, don't ask. Some saw rodentia while others saw toilets. In past dining experiences, "pork tenderloin" was seen as "fork tender"; "loins of beef" was guessed to be "groin relief"; and "cutlet of veal" became "cuticle meal."

No one, yet, has ordered the "Belize Smoked Gar and Tripe," which is, of course, "Please Don't Smoke Cigars or Pipes."

I didn't have my glasses. They were being passed around the table. They're trifocals, and everyone was just trying to somehow just use the bottom part to read the menu. Eventually we just asked the waiter to recommend something, and—given the noise level these days in trendy restaurants—it was as indecipherable as a subway train announcement. I had it anyway. May have been chicken.

My eyes were never any good. My senior year in high school it was discovered that I needed glasses and that I'd probably needed them for years.

The first thing that happened after I got them was that I broke up with my longtime girlfriend. Not because she didn't like guys with glasses, but because she was incredibly ugly! Had been for some time, I was told. Other things changed, too. I was surprised to see that there were actual *blades* of grass, which I had come to regard as some sort of indoor-outdoor yard goods from the Carpet Corral. I was further surprised to see that there were pertinent things written on the blackboard like "Test Tomorrow." Unfortunately it was my senior year and tough to pull up the old 1.9 average accumulated over three and a half years of fuzzy seeing and thinking.

Had this occurred today, I'm pretty sure I could have sued the school nurse for seventeen million dollars for failing to diagnose my visual learning disability, which kept me out of Harvard and off the board of Microsoft. Actually I *had* been diagnosed. Not as nearsighted but as a "jagoff," by Carl Nelson, Dean of Boys. Today they call my condition "Attention Deficit Disorder." They give you extra time on your SAT test and there are treatment programs. Actually there were treatment programs then, too, a graduated approach that began with asking you if you had "something funny to share with the entire class"; telling you to "shut up"; then "sit in the hall"; "report to the principal's office"; followed by "report to the principal's office and bring your coat." And finally, there was after-school detention, which for twelve years was a regular part of my day. In grammar school we emptied wastebaskets and cleaned erasers under the supervision of trained custodial personnel. In junior high and high school, we threw firecrackers inside the detention room, and climbed out on the third-floor ledge when the teacher was out so he'd return to find the room empty. No one in detention had glasses. We were good boys with bad vision. That's my theory.

I tried contacts. They were kind of experimental technology back in those days, fashioned from thick shards of jagged glass—or so it seemed. I can't use them now. My first contacts were so bad that thinking about wearing them now is like a flashback to 'Nam.

They're very popular these days with fiftyish women whose eyes are going but who think that glasses make them look like bread-baking grannies. They do make you look older, but sometimes wiser. Some TV personalities wear them just to make them look smarter. Geraldo does not wear them on his afternoon *Geraldo* show, where he interviews uneducated idiots, but he does wear them at night on his *Rivera* show, where he interviews educated ones like Alan Dershowitz.

Pushing fifty, Jody got contacts, the new soft disposables. And she looks like a younger woman, all right, albeit one that has just been maced.

Her red eyes water and she blinks 220 times per minute— more than Clinton lying on TV. At other times she just squints a lot. Part of the problem is she puts them in backwards. Reverses them, yes, putting the right one in the left eye, but also she actually puts them in backwards! Spends a lot of time looking for them on the backs of her eyeballs.

Bifocals became necessary in my early forties. I took it hard. They had that telltale line across the lens that lets the world know: this guy is old, really old. Little kids wear glasses, but only the aging wear bifocals. Just in the nick of time, medical science invented the blended lens with no visible line. Now I could look like a normal four-eyed geek instead of a really old four-eyed geek. I can now look up phone numbers but still dial them wrong.

When I was forty-five, the optometrist suggested . . . trifocals! These were no longer glasses; these were advanced vision systems.

With trifocals you get a small portion of the lens across the top to see things in the distance, a minute slice in the middle to see closer-range things like computer screens, a small portion at the bottom for reading, and little side panels that for some reason do . . . nothing.

You can always tell a person wearing trifocals even when they have blended lenses. They're the ones you see constantly tilting their heads up and down, this way and that, as they try to bring something—anything—into focus. Often they will squint and wrinkle their noses. They step warily off fuzzy steps and blurred curbs, objects that are out of focus because they're down there in the close-up, reading zone. Tennis with trifocals should be an event in the Special Olympics. It's almost impossible, as the ball whizzes from one zone to the next.

Now, a trip to the eyeglass emporium is an all-day affair, with more options to consider than the Caddy Seville.

The frames you get in the "under $100" package are so hideous they're almost cool. Almost. So you have to spend two hours considering thousands of expensive designer frames. That decision made, I then get trifocals. Side-panel pattern. Blended lens. Nonglare coating. Nonself-darkening. Lightweight. And ultrathin, because at this point my eyes are so bad normal lenses look like aquariums.

The tab is $650 ($475 plus the $175 free pair). Vision Express promises these ("under $100") glasses in one hour, but my Trained Vision Specialist told me they "should" be ready in two weeks—although they were not.

None of us can see anymore. Some are in denial. My friend Artie denied he needed glasses for years. He liked to enjoy a cocktail or two in the evening and then go boating, and one night he mistook an island for a shadow. Spent the night there shipwrecked.

Laser optic surgery is booming. Motel chains advertise large-type phone pads. Professional theft rings are dealing in designer eyeglass frames. At the mall they recently opened a new wing with about twenty new stores, and two of them are reading glasses stores right across from each other.

The Reading Glass store, part of a new nationwide chain, carries hundreds of designer frames. The glasses come in a variety of strengths, from minor magnification (+0.50), which allows you to actually see what you're ordering at the restaurant, to the +3.25s that allow you to identify hepatitis A bacteria on your strawberry-shortcake dessert.

At these new stores you can actually pay hundreds of dollars for reading glasses!—pretty much the same glasses my father-in-law buys out of a bin at the dime store for five bucks.

Their brochure trumpets "unbelievable savings." Indeed, how could anyone believe that spending two hundred dollars on five-dollar reading glasses is saving?

Like all specialty boutique stores—Just Tape!—Reading Glass takes a simple thing like magnifying glasses and runs up the cost with pricey, unnecessary options. Here you can buy designer frames for full-size or half-size reading glasses, single and multi focal, "sunreaders" and fold-up style.

Their brochure is in really, really small type. Smart. Their logo is two interlocking "Gs"—one the last letter in "Reading," the second the first letter in "Glass"—and the logo looks like one blurred "G." Smart.

"As a person ages," it reads, "the optical lens loses elasticity, making adaptation for close work more difficult"—which is why it can take two fifty-year-old people thirty minutes to clasp a necklace.

Finally, the brochure states in Bold Print: "Most people own more than one pair, allowing the wearer to leave glasses where they are most needed." Smart. And true. My wife has twelve pairs, none of which are where they are needed when they are needed.

She can't bring herself to wear them on a chain around her neck. That's *really* old.

Bad
Hair Decade

*O*verheard at Domenic and Pietro's Barber Shop: "At my age I've got more hair in my nose and ears than on my head."

At fifty, we're all follicly challenged. Our hair is either graying or gone. A generation is having a bad-hair era.

Some bald boomers tried for a while to make bald beautiful à la your Yul Brynners and your Michael Jordans. They were saying in typical boomer style, "Screw you, we don't have hair so we're redefining attractiveness!" Didn't work. Baseball cap sales soared.

Most bald guys have been bald for a while and seem thrilled that those of us with hair are having our own problem—graying. The baldies fight back with combovers, hairpieces, plugs, major transplants, the Hair Club For Men, reindeer antler extracts, and Popeil's "Amazing!" hair thickener—aka spray paint.

Combovers are the worst. No, wait. The worst is a remedy where you pull out your pubic hairs with tweezers—aieee!—theoretically rerouting hair nutrients to your head! If suggested, seek a second opinion.

Combovers still *look* worse. Combovers, of course, are where men comb hair from way down under their armpits or thereabouts up over their bald heads. They grow foot-long strands in that remaining horseshoe band of hair growing around the base of their skull, then swoop the strands up and over their barren heads. It's a lot to ask, like trying to make the Sahara look less "deserty" by calling FTD. Usually guys bring it up from the side, but some come up from the back to the front—for that sort of . . . tidal . . . look. In the most extraordinary cases, they'll bring the strand up and try to do a little Dairy Queen swirl thing on top of their skulls.

Hairpieces are not good either. They often get a little cockeyed, and really all you can do when you see that is just laugh right in the guy's face. The more serious the subject of his conversation the funnier it gets when the guy's hair is forty-five-degrees askew.

Some seem to purchase their toupees without regard to size. Or material. Polyester is great for boat hulls and leisure suits—try to imagine a worsted wool leisure suit? Ha!—but polyester is not the perfect choice when trying to duplicate human hair. The result is a hairpiece that looks as though it's been purchased in the automotive floor-mat aisle at Wal-Mart.

There were some quarter of a million hair transplants last year, where they take hair from the back of your head and move it up front. And then there are plugs, which to me always have the look of a guy trying to start an orchard with too little capital.

Sy Sperling's Hair Club For Men has always fascinated me. Where is it? And does it have a dining room, a golf course, and a swimming pool with lots of hairpieces floating around in it?

*   *   *

In ads and on TV, the ideal models and anchormen always have luxuriant manes. The bald guys? They're always fat and funny (like George on *Seinfeld*) and usually do the weather (like Al Roker, Willard Scott et al. ad nauseam).

A *Penthouse* study recently found that one quarter of American men would seriously consider swapping five years of their lives for a healthy head of hair. It further reported that men fantasize more about having good hair than they do about women. (I would question the latter finding were it not for the distinguished reputation enjoyed by the *Penthouse* Institute in the research community.)

At any rate, modern science cures all ills—as soon as they become boomers' ills. The boomers now have Rogaine. It comes in blue boxes for men, pink for women, and is scientifically proven to grow hair. It costs thirty dollars a month, but think of the potential sunscreen savings.

I see bald guys at the beach with thick hair all over their bodies and I wonder if they got the suntan lotion and the Rogaine mixed up. I have been thinking about a screenplay in the *Twister* or *Volcano* genre based on a massive Rogaine spill.

Sy Sperling bad-mouths the stuff. Scientists say Rogaine users should not expect spectacular results.

Users of Ron Popeil's GLH Formula 9 colored hair thickener, however, certainly *should* expect spectacular results— whether spraying it on their heads or on their patio furniture.

Edison notwithstanding, Ron Popeil is considered by me to be the greatest American inventor of all time, having given us a pantheon of "Amazing!" products, including: the legendary Popeil Pocket Fisherman; the Door Saver (an attractive air mattress you suspend from the side of your car to avoid scratches); the Egg Scrambler (scrambles eggs *inside* the shell!); and the

Food Dehydrator (turns any ten-dollar steak into ninety-nine cents' worth of beef jerky!)

On the infomercial, Ron Popeil holds an aerosol can of GLH ("Great Looking Hair") Formula 9 hair spray. Ron spent twenty-three million dollars on commercial airtime that he should have been given free as public service announcements. Because, like all of his products, GLH Formula 9 helps people. I mean, hell, the National Institutes of Health and the Center for Disease Control aren't doing squat about Male Pattern Baldness. Ron is. And any affliction that's that close to the brain, well, you'd better look after it pronto.

Ron says GLH makes bald spots disappear. The "suggested" (by someone) retail price on this amazing product is $110 a can. But! *If* you agree to tell just one person about it—promise?—you can have the can of GLH for $39.92! How does he do it?!

A woman in the infomercial audience says it best: "It's almost too good to be true!" And she doesn't know yet that she gets the fabulous Trim Comb (an amazing product that gives you a haircut while you're combing your hair) free! The man is just throwing in the GLH Finishing Shield for nothing! And the GLH Cleanser! And if you join his Hair Club for a dollar, you can get GLH aerosol refills for just twenty bucks! Ron! You'll go belly up with such shows of generosity!

The studio audience stampedes the stage to be treated by Ron. "I was waiting for a miracle and I found it," says one. Ron has to agree. He confidently approaches the bald spot on the back of the man's head, removes the cap from the aerosol can, shakes it, and begins spray painting the man's head in a more or less matching color.

What is GLH Formula 9? I don't know, but it's probably

a hell of a lot better than GLH Formula 8. You know how Ron's always working late in the lab. It may look like spray paint to the layman, but it is not. Ron says it's "colored hair thickener" that comes in nine colors, basic colors like black, brown, and yellow. No Williamsburg blue.

How long does it last? I sprayed some porch furniture with it a few weeks ago and it looks as good as the day I sprayed it.

I have a full head of hair (except for two V-shaped wedges at the top big enough to dock a couple of speedboats).

But it's turning from fiery red to a more blah shade, not graying so much as just kind of *fading*, which corresponds to a feeling I have generally.

The color's not really *bad*. Women still stop by my chair at the unisex hair cutter's to ask what color I use. The guy cutting my hair, Victor, always says "Clairol Number Forty-seven" to shut them up. (I hope for their sakes that Number Forty-seven isn't, like, *magenta*, but knowing Victor it probably is.)

I figure that I'm pretty well stuck with the color I've got. People who try to dye their hair to look like natural redheads usually have it come out the color of highway safety cones. They'll never get hit by cars jogging at night, that's for sure.

Many women go on search-and-destroy missions every morning in front of their mirrors, tearing out any and all gray hairs. They spend fortunes at the salons coloring gray—although my wife's friend, Kathleen, introduced her to a new cost-saving concept: coloring gray roots with a Magic Marker.

Even some manly men dye their hair these days. Republicans like Dole and Reagan. It's OK. Men have had Grecian

Formula on the shelves for years. But it perplexes me. It doesn't seem to come in colors. The guy on the box has black hair. Will it know I have red hair that's turning lighter? I don't think so.

My mustache is turning white. I'd buy some Just For Men beard and mustache dye if they had it in my color. Or I suppose I could shave it. They do say you look younger.

I realized recently that I'd originally grown it just to piss off an army sergeant, almost thirty years ago. Back then, I had to use an eyebrow pencil on my mustache because much of it grew in blond at first. I suppose if the sergeant had caught me at that I'd have been drummed out of the service. Time now, I guess, to buy another pencil.

Face Facts

My face is starting to resemble a scrotum sack. Wrinkled.

Crow's-feet? I have this recurring dream that hunters are walking across my face tracking giant emu.

The lines on my face lead to little red spots, like small towns on a map. Towns called Melanoma, Keratosis, and East Carcinoma—Mexican towns.

At fifty, you have a dermatologist. First-name basis. On my first visit, shortly after turning fifty, mine made me strip down and then she looked everywhere—places the sun doesn't shine. Why? Skin cancer lurks there, too. She stuck needles in me—excuse me, am I at an acupuncturist's?—before whittling off some tissue and sending it to the lab. Then she told me to come back and she'd burn some bad stuff off with lasers or with acid that could take graffiti off subway cars. It was such an attractive offer I didn't call back for a couple of years, so her office called me and demanded I return.

"At your age you have to look after these things," scolded my wife. The "at your age" hurt worse than the needles.

I called the doctor's office and talked to her associate. I told him that, yes, I knew skin cancer could kill you but that it just didn't really *seem* like it could, so I probably wouldn't be coming in. I explained that if the major artery in my neck were slit open and pumping blood onto the sidewalk, then I'd definitely see a doctor, but not for a little red spot.

"Well," he said, "even if it doesn't kill you, we might have to cut off your nose or your ear."

I went in. The doctor was about, oh, fourteen years old. They all look that way to me these days. I think I did refer to him once as Doogie. At least he spoke English. My last appointment was with a doctor who was wearing a sari and had to have a translator in the room. Another one was Chinese. It's one thing to have the Spanish-speaking guy at the McDonald's drive-through window give you fries when you asked for Sprite; it's quite another to have an Indian or Chinese doctor remove the wrong thing. "Remove 'wart'? Thought you said 'heart'. Thousand pardons."

Doogie stuck a needle in my stomach, removed a basal cell something or other, then he stuck a needle in my throat to deaden it and made some shavings for the guys at the lab.

He later sent me a registered letter instructing me to drop by and have my throat removed—or some portion of it. Maybe tomorrow.

He had other big ideas, too. Regarding the little red towns sprouting up on my facial map, he suggested something called Efudex and handed me a brochure. Picture One shows a guy before Efudex, Picture Two shows the guy undergoing treatment, and Picture Three shows the guy after treatment. The trouble is, the middle guy looks like he has used a napalm gel and a blowtorch to remove his facial blemishes. Or perhaps dipped his face in Strip-Ease furniture stripper. Or watched a couple of H-bomb explosions at close range. Jesus! The brochure tries to comfort me by saying "healing can be expected within one or two months"!

I tell the good doctor I'll get back to him. But I don't.

Removal of that button-sized red blemish cost $380. And six months later there is still a button-sized red blemish from the surgery in its place.

The doctor told me to stay out of the sun—forever—but I don't want to do that either. I need a little color. I am what Benjamin Moore would call "ceiling white," chalky white. When I lie on the beach with my eyes closed, the coroner's office comes by to see if the family needs any bereavement counseling or other assistance with the cadaver.

Pink pigs roll in mud not because they are filthy animals by nature, but because Coppertone doesn't make sunscreen for pigs. Thick black mud has an SPF rating of 1,000.

If humans were assigned SPF ratings mine would be 1,000, the whitest of the white man, the last to receive help through affirmative action. Casper is a 950. My skin is not considered opaque, although I was used in health class to identify organs.

Some peoples are equatorial, others descended from Mediterranean climes, others Scandinavian. My ancestors were CHUD (Cannibalistic Humanoid Underground Dwellers). My grandfather was the first in the family to have eyes.

Mine are blue, my hair red, my skin after two hours on a Florida beach, purple. I molt. At fifty, if I'm careful on vacations my face just takes on the look of a sun-dried tomato— same color, same texture. Think sunburned testicles.

I see people at the beach smearing on their SPF 50, putting zinc oxide on their noses, billed caps on their heads with the Lawrence of Arabia neck flap in back, sitting under their umbrellas. And I don't quite get it.

I tried a tanning booth once but I caught on fire. Really dry skin. Next I tried bronzing gels. Very tricky. The "Light" did nothing. "Dark" made me look like blackened redfish. "Medium" was just about right, but it was tough to keep the tan even. It piled up at knees and elbows and knuckles. Rather obvious. And my legs and arms would be tan but not my face. I was afraid to stain my face for fear it would look like a cheap Earl Scheib car paint job. Sometimes I forgot to wash my hands and there I was with brown palms. No one, of any hue, has brown palms.

The doctor suggested I use a moisturizer. I told him I already did, some cheap Oil of Olay knockoff sold at the food store: Oil of 7-Eleven, something like that. One of those that is also great for greasing bicycle chains and deep-fat frying.

"Perhaps a premium brand," he suggested, indicating that my current selection wasn't quite keeping pace with the ravages of aging. But Oil of Olay annoyed me. The youth fluid was endorsed by then tennis star Jennifer Capriati. She used it and managed to maintain her youthful appearance—even at sixteen.

Skin Spas

"Cement!?" Livia Sylva, World Famous Skin Care Expert, shrieked into the phone. "Darling, this is terrible and very ridiculous!"

Miss Livia, as she was known in her New York beauty clinic and spa, had heard of women putting all manner of garbage—old tea bags and potato peelings and other Dispose-All matter—on their eyelids, but this woman on the phone had put cement (great for highways and overpasses) on her face as a cosmetic mask and could not remove it. What could she tell this woman in cement? Dress up like a jockey and stand on the lawn?

"People are becoming more wrinkled and more desperate," said Miss Livia, who claimed, parenthetically, to also be a former Transylvanian Ping-Pong champion. "Someone suggests cement, they use cement. It is unbelievable, darling," she said in her best Zsa Zsa accent.

None of that hocus-pocus at the Livia Sylva Clinic de Beauté. Miss Livia did not use cement—or asphalt for that matter. Miss Livia's secret to eternally youthful-looking skin was the "proven" Rumanian bee pollen.

And where was it proven? Same place she was a Ping-Pong

champion. Why Rumanian bee pollen? "Because," she says dramatically in full Rumanian accent, "there is no pollen like Rumanian bee pollen."

In the heat of the baby boomers' frenzy to become wrinkle and stain free, facial salons are opening faster than Burger Kings and plastic surgeons offices. Madame Ilona of Hungary was offering whipped quail eggs and bull-blood wine. Not for brunch, for facials. Princess Marcella Borghese was partial to Italian mud.

Magazines for the well-to-do (who should be smarter) are chockablock with ads for Age Response System Gelee, Cellular Recovery Complex, Anti-Aging Cream, Line Preventor, Wrinkle Eradicator, Lift Serum, Biorhythmic Skin Care, Skin Response Hydrating Lotion, European Collagen Complex, Vasodilating Herb Extract, and Terme di Montecatini Mud—all at per-ounce prices rivaling beluga caviar. There is Activating Serum with Trace Elements (of what? Uranium 235?) and Embryo Cell Extract (what's the position of the Catholic Church on that?!).

Some doctors think it's a lot of poppycock. A few do not—especially those in the business. Claims are carefully worded, stating that the creams and lotions somehow "awaken the skin" or "help restore a balance to the skin" or even "encourage the skin." Let's go, skin! C'mon, skin! Don't give up!

Of naysayers who think most of these treatments don't really do much good, Miss Livia said with a sigh: "Yes, it is too bad people without knowledge"—and bee pollen—"get into this business. Clients are willing to try anything. They are combative. You wouldn't expect them to grow old gracefully."

There is much talk in the ads of mysterious beauty secrets of the pharaohs, of small Swiss clinics, and of Hungarian springs discovered by Romans.

Cleopatra, Miss Livia said, didn't know for sure about an afterlife, but stocked her tomb with bee pollen beautifier just in case. Eternity can seem like *forever* when you think you look like hell.

One salon was offering electroshock treatments to make the skin products penetrate deeper. (It might also eliminate depression associated with thinking you look old.) Others offer collagen and elasticin treatments, and one features a "volcanic ash mask" (that, frankly, looked like fireplace stuff to me).

One reflexology skin salon suggested pressing on the bottoms of the feet with a ballpoint pen each day, thereby causing better general health, a better complexion, and indelibly blue feet.

Miss Livia offered seaweed body wraps, but mainly she offered the Rumanian bee pollen.

"I believe in bee pollen," proclaimed a satisfied customer named Romy, emerging from a bee pollen facial (administered by a qualified "esthetician") and a "rejuvenating paraffin treatment" for the hands and throat.

"Miss Livia is an example for us all," the receptionist, Corrine, said in reverential tones. Miss Livia was immaculately and stylishly dressed and coiffed and she assured me that her wrinkle-free skin looked at least ten years younger than her age—although she was not about to say what that was.

Depends
on You

*A*n aisle named "Incontinence."

Sounds like a bad Tennessee Williams play, but these days aisles named "Incontinence" seem to be sprouting up in most big drugstores. Entire aisles brimming with Depend, Poise, Stayfree, and other disposable diapers. Scary canyons of adult diapers.

There are just so . . . many! Who are they all for? Ask not. They say they're targeting the "over fifty" market. *Us?!*

Adult diapers are now a billion-dollar business. There was an article in the paper the other day about one of the manufacturers building a big, new facility in Georgia to keep pace with the growing market. There was lots of enthusiasm on the part of executives about the growing loss of bladder control. Not theirs.

I see June Allyson hawking them on TV. She is painting and smiling and talking about Depends. Why is she painting? To show she can use watercolors with confidence, or what?

Jay Leno jokes about men drinking beer and watching TV football in Depends and never having to get up to go to the bathroom. And there was the joke about asking Dole if he wore boxers or briefs and Dole answering, "Depends." I gave a box to a friend on his fiftieth birthday. A lot of people didn't laugh.

Women have operations and implants for incontinence. Men friends have told me that the older they get the more they tend to dribble on their pants and on the floor when they pee.

Is *that* what they mean by the Golden Years?

One guy said he has been known to pee in the sink to alleviate the dribbling problem—a disgusting practice that women might be shocked to learn is not at all uncommon in crowded men's rooms at sports stadiums. Men!

Other men say they have to stand in front of a urinal forever these days before they start to go. Will I be taking magazines into the john to pee?

Buying Depends must be embarrassing, like buying condoms used to be. Now I always throw some condoms into the shopping cart hoping people will notice. The large. There are so many kinds of *adult* diapers now to choose from, what with all the different brands and special features like Easy Fit and Extra Absorbency. Will there be casual weekend Depends and black silk Victoria's Secret Depends?

Next to the Depends are the Pampers and Huggies the kids wear. I look at them and remember my little son sleeping in the same room with us at my aunt's house, where he rolled around all night in his crinkling, crackling plastic Pampers. He kept Jody and I awake, smiling. Will I crinkle too one day? Sweet Jesus. I ducked out of that aisle and headed for the "Forever Young" vitamin rack, pronto.

Spa
Weekend

Maybe *this* is the answer to aging. Seaweed wrap.

I am lying in state, on a padded, heated table in a soothingly warm, mocha-marbled, softly lit room filled with perfumed air and the dulcet tones of faint violins. The violins are playing "Ave Maria." You tell me: have I not died and gone to heaven?

But if that is true, why is my body smeared in gray-green seaweed goop, laminated in plastic, wrapped in a neck-to-toe electric blanket, and draped with towels. Could be a first step in the complex mummification process.

At first it seems totally absurd, then it feels good. Heavenly. I have seen no white light nor heard angels sing, but I have been concerned since I arrived at the Givenchy Spa, in Palm Springs, that I may have passed on, gone to a better place. And now I'm pretty sure of it. Although, there is also the possibility that I'm yet to be born. This *is* womblike, but better, with valet parking and better food. French cuisine and Russian caviar beat anything consumed through an umbilical cord.

My personal "esthetician," Carol, of Yorkshire, whipped up

and applied this seaweed pudding, and every so often she comes into the room to wipe my brow. The seaweed wrap has me concerned, worried every time the door opens, that in will burst a group of hungry Japanese businessmen with bottles of sake, chopsticks, soy sauce, and wasabi—for a little human sushi.

Carol explains that my body is releasing toxins—farewell, Absolut martinis! Au revoir large pepperoni and cheese!—through dilated pores, while soaking in "micronutrients." Welcome wee nutrients, one and all!

After forty minutes Carol pronounces me "done," and I open my eyes to make sure she isn't applying sour cream, chives, and Baco-Bits. She unwraps me and wipes the muck from my feet so I won't slip and slide on my way to the shower. After all, this is the same slime that makes trout fishermen fall in streams. Once at the shower I turn and look back at the table covered with soiled plastics and linens. It looks like a crime scene, only green, like the Mafia had rubbed out a martian.

This is the spa area, the treatment center, if you will, of the new Givenchy Hotel and Spa, which caters to The Catered To, many of them from LA.

Many of those who arrive in desperate need of rejuvenation and relaxation are surprisingly young, a lot of them thirty-somethings, completely stressed out by the backbreaking film industry, having to sit around and rack their brains, trying to figure out new ways for Arnold and Bruce and Sly to blow shit up in their next pictures.

Palm Springs itself is climatic heaven, guaranteeing 330 days of sunshine, albeit some of them at temperatures less suited to life than to cremation. The Givenchy grounds crew changes the sod to suit the season.

The air is clear and dry. At eighty-two degrees you can't

feel it, see it, or smell it the way you can in LA. This bothers city people who don't trust or believe in air they can't see— aero-atheists.

It is a special place, with street names like Frank Sinatra Drive and Gene Autry Trail, a place represented in Congress by the Honorable Sonny Bono, a place where Elvis still maintains a home.

The desert oasis is fast becoming something of a fountain of youth for concerned baby boomers, with several other spas, rows of cosmetic surgery facilities, and the home of the Life Extension Institute.

As we drive up to the Givenchy Spa, I am concerned that it might be one of these spartan training camps where they tell you you're fat, feed you Scotts Sun 'N' Shade grass seed, and take you on forced marches in the San Jacinto Mountains. Like boot camp but without the fun of sexual harassment. Just in case, I have emergency Snickers bars and vodka in the glove compartment should this thing get out of hand.

So, I am relieved to be greeted by two doormen and ushered into the lobby, where the first thing I spot is a piano bar.

You don't register! How gauche would that be? You are preapproved, or not, by this stage of the game. You are greeted by Rose Narva, the elegant proprietor, who lives here and tries to greet each guest personally—a nicety Mr. Marriott has given up on.

She leads Jody and me out the door on a perfect starlit evening, through formal gardens to the door of a forty-two-hundred-square-foot château. We mount the staircase to a vast two-bedroom suite. Our bedroom is large enough for arena football, decorated with antiques, and adorned with fresh-cut roses from the gardens below. There is a complimentary fruit basket so big you could hire a clerk and open a retail stand. There is a plate of sweets with "Bonne Nuit, Mr. and Mrs. Geist" written in chocolate on the platter. There is a canopied bed with eight pillows (silly, since we only use five), a large walk-in closet (which would be a $1,500 a month apartment in New York), a shower for about twelve (four heads!), more roses in the bath, a scale that registers about four pounds light, and a selection of Givenchy perfumes. Are you the type who takes home hotel amenities like soap and hair nets? Think U-Haul.

You tell me if I haven't died and gone to heaven. If I haven't, the bill itself will kill me.

Morning comes, but not until you're ready. (I think you just call the concierge.) We open louvered doors and see blue sky, the snowcapped San Jacinto Mountains, the formal gardens. We close the louvered doors and shake our heads in disbelief. You tell me.

We make coffee using our in-room coffeemaker. Nice, but then they do have those at some Holiday Inns these days. But at the HI the cups are Styrofoam. Here, the cups are Limoges. China. Limoges does not work in the Styrofoam medium.

We order room service: two granolas, one juice, one yogurt, and an espresso. Fifty-four bucks, plus tip. We think there's been a mistake, but don't have the fortitude to say so. The waiter might say we are the mistake. We keep our mouths shut and vow to live off the complimentary fruit basket from here on in.

We are concerned about our attire. Too much Gap, not enough Givenchy. I glance through louvered doors and size up the people walking about outside. Not bad, not too fancy, about like we're dressed. I feel better until I realize: these are custodial personnel.

We refer to our spa appointment cards, which were placed

on our pillows the night before, along with today's weather forecast ("Sunny, high 88 degrees") and chocolate-covered truffles. I'm so accustomed to staying in small-town motels without such amenities (although the Lebanon, Indiana, Holiday Inn did provide promotional, in-room flyswatters) that when I do stay somewhere nice I often wake up with chocolate mints stuck to the side of my head.

I am scheduled for a 9 A.M. massage. The prospect makes me tense. I am ticklish, for one thing, and unaccustomed to being stark—naked!—with someone's hands—all!—over me.

I have never had a massage (not counting that one time in Saigon), and to me they have always had a rather seamy connotation (counting Saigon). I recall massage parlors in Chicago during the seventies that were basically whorehouses, sometimes operating under rather ingenious guises. A couple of my favorites were the hot-tub showroom and testing center, and the stop-smoking center, where clients went into a room with a naked woman, and damned if the client did not, temporarily, stop smoking!

We dress as nicely as we can and head for the spa, a quick stroll through gardens of roses, boxwoods, lemon and olive trees, blossoming bougainvillea, palms, and water lilies.

The spa is a dazzling white building fronted by lofty palladian windows and slender columns and a parapet. In the atrium lobby we meet the spa director, a lovely woman named Chantal—not at all the dominatrix we'd worried about.

Chantal spoke not of regimens but rather of massages and the spa café and the boutique. Fitness shopping! Yes.

Here we split. Women go one way, men another. I was escorted to the locker room, where I undressed, placed my unworthy garments in a polished wood locker, and slithered into a Givenchy robe so plush I considered not stealing it for fear of grand larceny charges. The matching sandals were too small and caused me to shuffle about making that awful sound. I'm not a fan of open-toed footwear of any kind.

John, my masseuse, came by and we chatted on the way to the massage room. He pointed out the decorating—featuring Givenchy fashion sketches on the walls—and I quickly changed the subject to pro football and auto repairs so there would be no mistaking my sexual orientation. Under our current system, male masseuses are presumed gay until proven otherwise. Perhaps sensing my unease, John began talking about his wife and children.

Then he talked massages, offering me an entire menu, featuring the likes of the Relaxing Massage, Deep Tissue Massage, Sport Massage, and a dozen others.

There was Foot Reflexology, which involved grape-seed oil and stimulation of pressure points to affect the organs. But it did not specify which organs, and besides I'm too ticklish.

The Aromatic Massage with Essential Oils promised something peculiar, "harmonization of bodily functions," which I could only assume had something to do with making music with belches and farts. No?

There was Lymphatic Drainage, which sounded gross. And there was the Slimming Massage, which promised "remodeling" of the body through a restructuring of supporting tissue and enhancing the suppleness of my connective tissue with Givenchy Body Shaping Massage Cream. It sounded like something you would do to your house.

There was Pressure Therapy, involving inflatable pads and an air compressor, but I worried I might wind up in the Macy's Thanksgiving Day Parade. And, Shiatsu, but I don't like dogs.

So, we settled on the straightforward Swedish Massage, which he described as a "noninvasive" massage. Invasive?! Inside-out massage? Leave that to the proctologists, buddy.

In a leap of faith, Jody went with the Slimming Massage. Her masseuse explained that these work if you exercise and don't eat fat. (So does mah-jongg.) He first applied a potion made up of "secret herbs and rare spices" (Kentucky Fried Chicken batter?) plus a special patented ingredient that "re-elasticizes" the skin. The masseuse explained that it "detoxes" the area (maybe they should send Hubert de Givenchy to Chernobyl) so fat globules don't stick to the skin or membrane covering muscle. Then he massages the fat to break it up, separate it from skin, and smooth it out. That's his story.

We stroll past the fitness center on our way to lunch. There are never any lines at the fitness center, no one in the yoga center, no one crowding around the mountain hiking sign-up sheet. They're all at the bar or in the restaurant.

Somewhere I read that you're supposed to have seven—seven!—servings of fruits and vegetables every day, so I order a mimosa. Seven! Better give me two mimosas. And I'll have the tuna, which arrived so spectacularly handsome that I actually took its picture. (Do stop over and see my vacation slides.)

We dined alfresco on the patio under an umbrella. There was one moment of tension when a mild argument broke out at the next table over beluga versus sevruga. They ordered both. And champagne. I noticed that both looked in great physical shape and made a mental note of their diet.

My kind of spa. In the French tradition, as they say, meaning: the help does the heavy lifting here, not you. No pampering, no gain. Self-indulgence, not sacrifice.

We looked out upon the tranquil gardens with clients strolling to and fro in their white robes, giving the place the look of a sanitarium of some sort—or perhaps a college for boxers. Or heaven. You tell me. And pass the foie gras.

But enough of reverie. Time for our next procedure. The facial. Monique, just in from Nice, performed Jody's facial; Sheryl did mine. My first. By now *I* was starting to talk about decor, which scared me enough that I skipped Introductory Makeup and Eyebrow Shaping. Sheryl cleansed my face—you never just *clean* anything; at these prices, you *cleanse*—with lotions and a brush before giving my kisser a collagen spray. At the car wash this would be the Deluxe. Then they brought in the Esty 2000 humidifier, a big spritzer, while applying creams and a mask. The facial was an unexpected pleasure, as she augmented it with sumptuous neck and shoulder massaging and rubbing of the chest. Stimulating, almost uplifting at times. Sheryl left the room while I gave in to a mimosa-induced nap.

Jody's facial wasn't *that* good, but she reaped some of the benefits of my stimulation as we returned to our room for a nap. Had to rest up. It was almost seaweed hour.

The spa-treatment menu was high on seaweed: "This wrapping treatment can be used to reshape the body, slimming its outline to regenerate well-being and stimulate the metabolism." I'm certain.

Jody took notes on her seaweed wrap: "Nudity really offends me at this age. I'm handed a paper thong to wear and the rest is public. She covers every square inch of me with the thick, smelly green goo, all the while talking casually about her home in Maine. I have trouble being a good listener.

"She flips me over and asks if I mind if she does my bosom.

I'm flattered to be considered bosomy and consent. She finishes with the bottoms of my feet. My feet have been through a lot today and are cracking. All the better to drain the toxins.

"After being thoroughly coated in slime, I'm wrapped in Saran wrap, then covered in thick towels. The heat of the electric table is being trapped and I feel a long, menopausal hot flash coming on. To my surprise my therapist pulls out a down coverlet to ensure a slow bake. She excuses herself and I find myself alone, immobile, and listening to soft orchestra music. I thought I saw the long tunnel with a bright light at the end.

"When I was medium rare, the coverlet, towels, and Saran wrap were peeled away and I was looking weird. I would have fit in well in the Galápagos reefs, but I was led to the shower and hosed off. Voilà! The new nontoxic, elasticized me."

We meet in the lobby. I actually do feel (somehow) invigorated from the primordial green goo; Jody feels so relaxed she can barely stand.

Chantal rushes over, looks at us, and says: "You are glowing!" She meant it as a compliment, but it is just not something you say to people like us who live in New Jersey amongst the radon and toxic-waste sites and nuclear power plants.

As the sun sets over the San Jacinto Mountains, I'm off to: My First Manicure, which sounds like the title of a children's book in a prep-school library.

I'm apprehensive. Will the manicurist chastise me and slap my cuticles? She sensed right away this was my first: the teeth marks, the tears, the fifty-year cuticle buildup, the overall . . . stubbiness. She sighed and began working long into the evening. She asked if she might put a hint of color on the nails and I said she might not. She put on a clear polish—but high gloss. I started talking about pro football again.

We had dinner with Rose Narva, and her husband, Bill Narva, a retired admiral, a dermatologist, and a man who pulls no punches.

"Rose doesn't let me in the spa building," he says, "because I really don't believe that stuff. If your skin allowed toxins to flow in and out the way they say, we'd all be dead by now."

Rose said they have a lot of postoperative clients recuperating after visits to local cosmetic surgeons. She said her clientele is younger than she expected: in the thirty-five to fifty-five range.

We repaired to the Library Lounge for some healthful scotch, then it was off to bed. Had to get up early for room service: crab-cake eggs benedict. We prayed our slimming, shaping massages would hold up against the onslaught of calories.

At 10 A.M. we reported to the spa for our Givenchy Exclusive, the grand finale, a two-hour coup de grâce.

It began with a body scrub. Again, a first for me. Suffice it to say, power tools were necessary. Carol applied a scrub that she said contained seeds. What kind of seeds? "Plastic seeds," she explained. (I had no idea that plastic was actually grown.) She worked my body sector by sector, expertly flipping the little ten-inch square towel this way and that, just so, so as not to reveal my privates, applying the scrub, then using the power scrubber. Serious exfoliation. Agent Orange–strength.

"When I was on the table getting power buffed by Monique, it reminded me we need the kitchen floor refinished," Jody said.

While they cleaned up the room in preparation for the next step, I was sent to the showers, then the sauna, then the steam room. They claim that a sauna in combination with cold showers may enhance the body's immune defenses—and, of course, may not. They say that steaming and baking opens pores and facilitates an outpouring of toxins. In any case, we're paying to perspire—something that would make my hardworking father roll over in his grave.

The last steam room I'd visited was at the Tenth Street Baths, an out-at-the-elbows Russian "spa" in New York City, where blimplike Russian men go to be flogged with oak-leaf brushes, sit in unbearable heat, and be doused with buckets of ice water—after which they drink shots of vodka, eat pickled herring, and nap on old, stained mattresses. It does not appear to be slimming.

Step two of the Exclusive was what Jody referred to as the lamb-chop treatment, being covered in mint-green jelly, wrapped, and baked. Again I envisioned cannibalistic businessmen on expense accounts bursting in with knives and forks. Instead it was only Carol, who unwrapped me and left while I showered. Monique always helped my wife shower, washing her back and such, and Jody always vowed never to do this again without dieting first. When it was over Jody described her skin as inhumanly soft, "like Velveeta."

I was offered the Marine Mud Wrap, but I wanted to leave the Marines out of this, even though my gut might be referred to as Pork Chop Hill. I opted for the Herbal Wrap. Mint jelly, Saran wrap, slow bake. By now, the meat is starting to separate nicely from the bone.

Then it was time for another shower. My forty-fifth! I was beginning to worry that all this might prove counterproductive, my body bloating up like a floater dipped from the Hudson River by the NYPD.

The final stage involved a coating of moisturizer, more Saran wrap, and an unforgettable water-jet massage. Lying flat and wrapped, a row of powerful, almost bruising water jets (men *must* lie on their backs) begins beneath your feet and works its way up to the neck, then returns back down again—repeating this over and over until you're beaten tender like a cheap steak at the Sizzler.

What price beauty? The bill for this two-night, two-day stay would run about $550 for the room—although Rose could have charged us $4,000 for two-thirds of the château; about $300 for meals; about $600 for spa treatments; and $150 for tips; for a total of about $1,600.

We wondered if a Freemen approach would work here at the Givenchy Spa: holing up in the château, saying we do not recognize Rose Narva's authority, refusing to check out, paying for things with bad checks the way the Freemen did, and demanding continued facials and seaweed wraps if authorities didn't want this thing to turn ugly.

Finally we hit the road. As we drove into the LA traffic I swear I already felt the creases reappearing in my face. I thought of the spa shape-up treatments, then compared that to the hell we used to go through to get into shape for high school sports with twice-a-day practice sessions, running laps, running wind sprints until we were sick to our stomachs—when all we had to do was take a slimming, restructuring seaweed wrap, drink champagne instead of Gatorade, and eat caviar.

What fools we were.

Warning Signs of the Onset of "Middle-aged" Grumpiness

- Tell Starbucks' clerk to cut the "half-caf/half-decaf double mocha latte" bullshit and give you a cup of coffee
- Advocate pretrial hangings of O. J., McVeigh, and Kosinski
- Believe we should shoot the Freemen, then hold thorough discussion of their (cheap) political philosophy
- In discussion of the latest mass murder, find yourself siding with the disgruntled postal worker
- On first-name basis with your proctologist
- Buy a handgun to "change channels" next time *Jenny Jones Show* comes on
- Remove car seat belts with hedge clippers because they're too uncomfortable to sit on
- Open child-proof aspirin bottles with hammer
- Tell parents with baby in restaurant that you'd rather see "No Children" than "No Smoking" sections
- Tell teens "rap artist" is an oxymoron
- Consider greater than 50 percent of your fellow motorists "assholes"
- Trip a running child
- Tell the car dealer who wants 40Gs for a Toyota "I thought *we* won the war"

204

- Feel it necessary to actually *tell* young people that characters on *90210* and *Baywatch* can't act
- Believe Rodman should be earning quarters in carnival side-show tents, not millions in the NBA
- Recently yelled "get off my lawn, you little bastards"
- Tell Native-American protestors to "shut up and deal"
- Consider microbrewed raspberry wheat beer to be complete bullshit
- Free-range chicken, also bullshit
- Bottled water, radon, the information superhighway, arugula, Gulf War (syndrome, war, parades)—all bullshit
- Believe cab drivers ought to know location of the Empire State Building (or Chicago's Sears Tower, or the Los Angeles airport, etc.) as well as the location of the brake pedal on American makes
- Come home with "Kill 'Em All And Let God Sort 'Em Out" tattoo
- And, taking a look at current elected officials, recent jury verdicts, and most popular TV shows, books, and movies—you're pretty sure democracy is a failed experiment

Not Much
Fun Fair

*I*thought it might lift my
spirits to go to a Fun Fair.

"CELEBRATION 50+," read the newspaper
headline. "The Best Years of Your Life! A Lifestyle Expo for
the Age 50+ Population."

They always say you don't have to be young or drinking to
have a good time, so I drove on down to the big Fun Fair at the
Meadowlands Hilton, in Secaucus, New Jersey, where the ma-
jestic New Jersey Turnpike cuts through marsh grass and cat-
tails sprinkled with waterfowl and the occasional steel-belted
radial.

It was a perfect fall day, warm and sunny, with lots of revelers up for a good time heading to the Fun Fair.

Admission was three dollars, so there was a *little* trouble
right off.

"Don't you have a group rate?" snapped one woman.

"For groups of twelve or more," explained the man at the
registration table.

"Well, I brought five," said the woman, perhaps thinking
she wouldn't have bothered picking up a couple of these old
biddies if she'd known they didn't count toward some discount.

"Sorry," the man replied. Five didn't cut it.

"Senior discount?" pressed the woman.

The registrar laughed. He probably figured giving a senior discount at a seniors fun fair was sort of like giving a student discount at the school cafeteria.

The Fun began right when you walked through the door, where us funsters were met by the musical stylings of a group called Justa Buncha Banjos. Ever heard of 'em? Now, I have never personally appreciated banjo music, have you? But I realized that now that I was "50+" I'd better start.

I sat down (seniors, I was learning, will watch *anything* if they get to sit down) and attempted to learn to appreciate this group, which was bedecked in red and white striped shirts—very nice—and playing a tune entitled "Hello." Do you know it? It goes: "Hello, what a wonderful word, hello" and so on.

I wondered if any of these guys were at Woodstock. And I wondered: if Hendrix were still alive, would he be up there singing "Hello" and setting his banjo on fire?

A fellow was passing out "Seniors Love Karaoke Music!" flyers with the phone number of his mobile karaoke outfit. Another man asked when the Pierce Arrows barbershop quartet was scheduled to perform. I could see that as a new fifty-pluser I had a lot of learning to appreciate to do.

"If You're Not 55, You'll Wish You Were!" read an intriguing sign for the Four Seasons Adult Community. I thought that booth looked like Fun, figuring an "adult community" might be like "adult books" or "adult movies." Alas, it did not mean a community of nubile neighborhood nymphos, but rather a community of people over fifty-five years of age. Too bad, but it could have been worse. It could have been a neighborhood of over-fifty-five nymphos.

These adult communities used to bug me. The ones where grandchildren practically have to visit their grandparents through bullet-proof glass, like the wives and girlfriends in those prison movies. Damned near. You know, the adult communities where rules specify that children can stay no more than two days, cannot make sounds, must be on a leash, cannot play on the grass, and cannot swim in the pool except during Early Bird Special hour at the Sizzler steak house. Lately, however, now that my kids are elderly, I have come to think that perhaps children really should be licensed at age eighteen or twenty before they can go on airplanes, in restaurants, and elsewhere in the public sector.

A number of adult communities were represented at the Fun Fair, including some in "Genuinely Affordable" (Highly Unbearable) central Florida, and some for "higher functioning adults" like myself. Nice to be an HFA, I suppose, but I'd really rather not be on their radar screen at all.

I actually kind of liked the idea of moving into Holiday Manor, for lower functioneers, because it offers daily housekeeping, cooking, and home maintenance. Not later. *Now.*

Talk about Fun! At the Equitable investments booth you could putt a golf ball and possibly win a free lottery ticket. Smith Barney investments was right next door.

There was all sorts of free giveaway promotional-item stuff, and these seniors were raking it into their complimentary plastic bags like house burglars. Ever watch a busload of seniors hit a casino buffet? Looks like something you'd see on *Wild Kingdom.*

Donald Trump knows his market. His Atlantic City casinos were passing out coveted buffet coupons. Merv Griffin's Resorts casino was holding a drawing for two free tickets to its "Funderful" floor show. I've seen these shows and always assumed they were for the visually, auditorially, and mentally impaired.

I copped a free bag of Lipton's Soothing Moments Gentle Orange Herbal tea. Imagine? A tea with "soothing," "gentle," and "herbal" all in the same name. Stuff had to have Valium in it. It's a new product aimed at the aging, but frankly I don't really need any more tranquilizing in my life. I need a six-pack of Jolt cola.

There *were* free cans of Canfield's Diet Cherry Fudge soda, which seemed pretty out of control for this occasion. I mean, where's the Sustacal and the Ensure Light?

Three women were helping themselves to free tubes of Sensodyne toothpaste "for sensitive teeth," and free samples of Glide dental floss and a competitor named Reach. There were free Butler G-U-M toothbrushes too. Gums were big at the Fun Fair. Scare pamphlets were circulated by the makers of Listerine: "Three out of four adults have gingivitis! Do you?"

Rats! I came too late for the dental implant seminar.

At various points you could get your vision, hearing, and blood pressure checked. Free. That was sort of fun. You know, like a Health Fun Fair?

Yours for the asking: free copies of *Seniors Today* magazine, with information on where to see a free movie at 1 P.M. on Wednesdays; what time the Early Bird Specials begin at the Green Kitchen restaurant (4 P.M.); a coupon for a free hearing test at the Beltone hearing-aid store (consumer tip: you may not pass); and an ad for an Alfred's Senior Citizen Club nine-day bus tour to Florida. Hope that one's not booked.

Palisades General Hospital was here. Hey, I thought this was supposed to be *Fun*! No funeral homes, thank God. Come to think of it, I hadn't noticed Dr. Kevorkian's van in the lot either. (Doctor Jack! You gotta make these trade shows!)

A store that sells magnifying glasses was represented. "I could use one of those," said a woman who looked to be in her seventies. "I'm getting so I can't read menus anymore."

"Me either," I said, and realized that I was starting to fit right in. We chatted about the menu problem and then I said I had to be going.

"Don't go now," she said, "you'll miss the Harmoneers." I gathered that they were another singing group I'd be missing— not to mention the "Aging Eye" seminar that was about to begin.

"Unfortunately I do have to go," I explained. "I work."

"You *do*?!" she replied, seemingly quite surprised.

Jesus, how old did she think I *was?*

The Fun Fair had not been *Fun*, certainly, but that is probably another sign of age: my thinking a Fun Fair could actually *be* fun. A few years ago I would have known better.

On the roof level of the Hilton parking garage it was warm and sunny, like Florida, and two crotchety motorists were honking at one another, for no apparent reason in the world.

The Memory Center

"Honey, I'm calling from a pay phone. I can't remember the address of The Memory Center. . . . 150 White Plains Road? OK. . . . Wait! 150?"

I was driving in the car (possibly with my turn signal still on) when I heard a commercial on the radio for this new place called The Memory Center, catering to "Alzheimer's sufferers" and "baby boomers."

First I thought, "Gee, I never really considered boomerism a disease before," and then I thought, "My God, how the American entrepreneur is on top of things! It makes you proud."

Boomers are losing their minds by the millions, and now all they have to do is dial 1-800-IS-RELIEF. But how the Memory Center will garner business when customers can't remember the phone number is beyond me. I jotted the number down, called in, and (after that refresher call home) stopped by.

I didn't know what to expect. Would the place be filled with customers racking their brains to fill out the name, address, and phone number cards? Would there be a drive-through window where patients could get $9.99 electroshock jolts to jog their memories?

The Memory Center turned out to be in a suburban office building, not some free-standing Foto-Mat or Burger King roadside franchise deal. Inside were clients with electrodes sticking out of their heads, others hooked up to biofeedback machines, still others taking written memory tests and playing computer memory games.

Staff doctors were consulting colorful "Topological Brain Maps" drawn up for individual clients, and studying computer screens showing clients' brains, with color-coded alpha, beta, delta, and theta waves running though them. Blood, hormone, and genetic testing is also performed here.

"We hope to have a hundred of these centers across the country in three or four years," Jonathan Raven, CEO of Memory Centers of America, effervesced.

He knows all about the tsunami wave of baby boomers and the money to be made from our falling apart at the seams right on schedule. He was previously president of one of those glasses-in-one-hour outfits. "Did you know," he said, "that 95 percent of people over age 45 need glasses? Death, taxes, and glasses—it's that certain."

"And this has the same demographics!" he exclaimed—not quite rubbing his hands together, but almost. He seems genuinely pleased and downright optimistic about the prospect that our brains are all about to go.

He's 46 years old himself and is pretty sure it's already happening to him. "I dial someone on the phone," he laughed, "and when they answer I can't remember who I've called." Easy for him to laugh; he holds a lot of stock in the burgeoning mental-lapse industry.

"Or I'll meet someone and three minutes later I swear I can't remember the guy's name," Mr. Raven said with a chuckle. I chuckle along with him, a bit nervously, while trying to come up with his. Raven. (I keep hoping he'll quote something so I can write "quoth Mr. Raven," but he doesn't.) "You know," he continueth, "boomers smoked a lot of marijuana way back when, and studies documenting the adverse effects on the brain are now showing up. I inhaled. I admit it. I'm not running for anything."

He said some people come into the Center and are advised that they don't really have much of a problem. He thinks we all have too much information bombarding us these days to remember it all. "Attending," he said. "That's a key concept." He said we take in lots of information without fully "attending" to it, so we aren't really forgetting some of these things because we never really bothered to store them in our memory banks in the first place.

"There is a stigma to having your brain checked," he admitted, but adds that the Center does have a way to keep this out of our personal medical files and thinks the stigmas can be overcome. "After all," he said, "this is the Wellness Generation. Look at the things boomers are already doing: hair transplants, liposuction, face-lifts, Rolfing . . . penile implants!

"We check our hearts, our lungs, our cholesterol—it's about time we started checking our brains."

Indeed. It all sounded sensible to me, but then, maybe my brain is shot.

"It's the last taboo," chimed in Dr. Islah Ahmed, a neuropsychiatrist on the staff. "Asking someone if he's checked his heart is a nice thing to ask. Ask him if he's checked his brain, and it's an insult."

Dr. Ahmed can relate to boomers coming into the Center. He keeps locking his keys in his car.

"People don't check their brains," added Dr. Turan Itil,

who runs this particular Center, "because the brain does not produce pain. You don't go to the doctor because your brain hurts. Also, it does not kill you. It's not considered a critical organ."

Should boomers be concerned about memory loss?

"Memory disturbance!" corrected Dr. Itil. "We don't like to say 'loss.' "

"We prefer 'forgetfulness,' " said Dr. Ahmed. "It's more benign."

"Whatever you call it," I said, "I'm just talking here about minor things, things that happen to me, like always forgetting where I put my car keys or meeting someone ten times and not being able to remember his name. At 50, that's all just common."

Silence.

"Common?!" blurts out Dr. Itil. "Not so common!"

I was taken aback.

"All your life you've had a good memory," he said, "and suddenly you can't remember things? This is not common."

"But," I retorted, "none of my friends who are fifty can remember anything either."

"Bring them in," Dr. Itil stated solemnly.

It suddenly dawned on me that perhaps our whole town is built on a toxic-waste site or something, and I imagined thousands of us boarding bus convoys to the Memory Center. (Or! Maybe I $hould open one in town.)

"But," I said, "I don't need an evaluation or anything, do I?"

"If," answered Dr. Itil, "you plan to live just ten more years, then the answer is no."

Sixty?

"But," he continued, "if you plan to live longer, then yes,

because the memory loss could be a warning of worse things to come, and we can intervene."

Yikes. I'm not ready for this. What with my deteriorating eyesight, distending waistline, diminishing libido, and all the rest, all I need right now is an evaluation telling me I'm headed for dementia and I'm calling Kevorkian for a ride home in the van.

Besides I didn't have the $600 for a thorough checkup (without blood tests). It's not covered by health insurance because then it becomes part of your medical history and nobody wants a doctor writing "CRS—Can't Remember Shit!"—on his or her medical record.

What do doctors at the Memory Center prescribe when you can't remember stuff?

"It depends," said Dr. Itil. "Most cases can benefit from the over-the-counter plant extract ginkgobiloba."

"Excuse me?" I say.

"You don't know this?!" Dr. Itil erupts.

"Maybe I forgot," I said apologetically, and explain that "Plant Extracts" is not one of my stronger *Jeopardy!* categories.

"It's extract of the ginkgo tree," he explained. "We have done extensive studies. It's a proven cognitive-disturbance treatment. We might also prescribe vitamins, antioxidants, or food supplements, as well as biofeedback sessions and brain gymnastics."

How about those old tricks like remembering Bob's name by labeling him "Bald Bob" in your memory bank?

"Not too professional," said Dr. Itil.

Treatment varies, he said, because of the multitude of factors that can cause memory disturbance.

"A patient," he said, "might have vigilance disturbance and be half asleep in the middle of every afternoon."

"Could you repeat that?" I ask (at 3 P.M.). Should I tell him about the siestas on my office floor? No.

"Or a patient might be tired all the time," he explained, "and need alpha-wave biofeedback." Definitely not, nothing about the naps.

"Or something like testosterone deficiency caused by male menopause could be the memory problem," said Dr. Itil. I tell him I can't remember the last time I had sex and it's confusing to me if this is a memory problem or if it's been so long that The Amazing Kreskin couldn't remember it. Either way, a testosterone booster shot couldn't hurt.

If you have serious problems the doctors prescribe drugs that can help. "I am taking some drugs and I can remember more phone numbers," Dr. Itil said. Drugs replacing phone books. This must be the nineties.

They recommend regular brain checkups at three-to-six-month intervals. Since there is currently no such thing as a brain checkup, their recommendation to have one every three to six months seems tantamount to my barber recommending a haircut after every meal.

It's time to be going. I'm concerned that if I tell them one more thing about my memory loss—disturbance, I mean—that they're just going to commit me on the spot as a Memory Center inpatient.

I imagine myself taking the battery of scientific tests: written, computer, EEG, hormone, genetic, and all the rest here at the Center, then being called before a panel of the doctors for my diagnosis. Dr. Itil would be at the head of the conference table: "Mr. Geist, after thorough evaluation, our team of neuropsychiatrists has come to the medical conclusion that You Can't Remember SHIT!" And they'd all have a good laugh.

By coincidence, just then Mr. Raven interrupted my daydream, jovially asking me, "Have you ever heard of CRS?"

"Of course," I answer. "I have a friend who's a doctor."

"Well," he said, consolingly, "we all have a touch of it."

We bid farewell and I went out into the parking lot to begin the search for my car.

Romance—Is That a Hot Flash or Are You Just Glad to See Me?

omen complain that the thrill is gone, that by age fifty men have become unromantic clods.

I say they're wrong. I say that's incredibly age-ist. I say we have *always* been unromantic clods, that despite thousands of years of attempted domestication, men remain insensitive slobs, better kept outdoors.

We know we have feelings because sometimes we hit our thumbs with hammers, but there is scant evidence to suggest much beyond that.

Women are different. Women watch soap operas and read Barbara Cartland romance novels by the millions. They buy "I Can't Believe It's Not Butter" spray because Fabio tells them to. And they make pilgrimages to Madison County (Iowa) to see the bridges and eat in the diner where Robert ate, and take pictures of the pay phone Robert used, and see the kitchen where Robert and Francesca danced—they're fictional, folks, fictional!—and buy souvenir pieces of boards from one of the bridges, and bottles of sand from beneath it. I saw these women doing it. Thousands of 'em. Why was I there? The John Wayne Museum's in the same town. That's my alibi.

At fifty, all women dare ask of us is that we try to act a little romantic a couple times a year: on our wedding anniversaries and on Valentine's Day.

At this age, some of us are running up against twenty-fifth (!) wedding anniversaries. This is big. We're not talking the Sizzler or Red Lobster here. We're talking serious business, serious money. We're talking restaurants with tablecloths and salad forks and No Nachos! We're talking about ordering stuff you'll have to point to because you can't pronounce it.

We're talking silver, certainly, but more than that, we're talking jewelry. Real jewelry. If you've been caught passing her zirconium before, don't chance it again, not on this occasion. If you find it necessary to purchase the jewelry at Service Merchandise, go to a nice mall and try to find a Tiffany's bag to put it in.

We are talking champagne, champagne not purchased at the Beer Hut, perfume not purchased at Wal-Mart, flowers not purchased at a grocery store. Women hate it when there's a "Produce" sticker on their bouquets.

We may even be talking one of those "Romantic Getaway Weekends" advertised in the paper. Be careful. These are scams set up to fill motels on weekends when business travelers are home. Of course, as a man, I consider anything romantic or sentimental to be a scam—like Mother's Day.

At least make sure the Romantic Getaway is in a semi-romantic neighborhood, and not at the end of airport runway 4L or something. We made the mistake of taking advantage of a Romantic Getaway Weekend offer at a Holiday Inn that turned out to be in an industrial neighborhood of a blue-collar Chicago suburb. All there was to do was watch the eighteen-wheelers unload at the Kmart warehouse across the street.

And of course, there's Valentine's Day. Valentine's Day is to men as Wrestlemania is to women. Nothing!

And before we go any further here, I would like to say that scheduling Valentine's Day in February wasn't exactly the smartest idea in the world. February is not a time for romance, but rather, psychologists suggest, a time for clinical cabin fever and screaming at one another. Particularly in northern climes. I mean, even a *young* man's fancy doesn't turn to thoughts of love till spring. With a guy my age it can take till, like, Labor Day.

It isn't always pretty when once or twice a year we're called upon to play the romantic lead. Men know Valentine's Day is a holiday, and we know it's America, so we know we have to *buy* something. But what?

Our romantically impaired gender is thrown on the mercy of the business sector. And what do the newspaper ads suggest? Let's see, now: Tiffany's is offering a heart-shaped diamond for forty grand. Nah.

Other Valentine's Day ads advise us:

"Say It with Pizza"

"This Valentine's Day, Give Her a Whirlpool Multi-cycle Washer"

"Nothing Says I Love You Like Our Succulent Veal Parmigiana"

"Surprise Her with a GE Spray Steam and Dry Iron"

*   *   *

A word to the wise: Do Not turn you back on your Valentine after surprising her with a steam iron. The surprise may be on you.

Another ad suggests we give our Valentine a nice set of steel-belted radials (apparently to prove we are concerned for our love's safety). Several highly unromantic products are using this "caring" approach. But know this: there are a lot of men out there sitting on the floor with their legs crossed in group therapy, saying: "I don't know why she left me, I gave her everything: a First Alert Smoke Detector for Christmas . . ."

I have seen Valentine's Day ads suggesting Monroe shock absorbers and Scotch tape as appropriate gifts for that special (very!) someone. Could be kinky.

Most men fall back on the old standbys. We'll realize around 4 P.M. that it's Valentine's Day and pick up flowers—the picked over, browning ones—on the way home from work.

Or some perfume. I bought perfume once. Cologne, actually. At Walgreens. "Evening in Paris." For my mom. Three decades ago. *Loved* it. *Still* has it. *All* of it.

The drawback to perfume is that you have to walk down that department-store aisle and be set upon by platoons of women spritzing you with perfume like they were some sort of odor-response team and you were the emergency. Not to mention: this stuff can cost hundreds of dollars an ounce! Bijan: $350.

That "best things come in small packages" concept does not appeal to unromantically inclined guys like myself who believe that buying in bulk best proves our love. We want Perfume-in-a-Drum or a gargantuan box of candy from Home Depot that has to be removed from the shelf with a forklift. A big seller now is the *four-pound* heart-shaped box. But: will you want to *live* with this woman after she eats fifty bucks' worth of chocolates? Well, how big is your apartment?

Restaurateurs suggest taking your valentine out for dinner. But this too can be tricky for those unwise in the ways of love. The whole thing backfired on a friend of mine who looked into his valentine's eyes over cappuccino and purred: "I think I can write this off." Actually, it was he that was written off.

A Valentine's dinner once backfired on me as well, and to this day I still don't know if it was just the whole drive-through window thing per se, or if it was holding those greasy bags on the lap of the new dress she bought for the evening. Women! I tell ya.

Sexy lingerie is the hottest new Valentine's Day gift. But this is no easy buy. I have to look around to see if anybody's watching before I walk into a women's lingerie department. My palms get sweaty. I mean: isn't it *against the law* for men to be in a women's lingerie department?

And know this: your Victoria's Secret GC510-790 stretch-lace merry widow with underwire cups, detachable garters, matching bikini, and stretch stockings may not look *exactly* the same when modeled at home as it did on the high school senior wearing it in the picture at the store. Could be the lighting.

And those things look terribly complicated. I certainly wouldn't buy them if I was in a hurry. Assembly must take hours, what with all the interlocking systems of snaps and garters and belts and pulleys and whatnot. It makes putting that swing set together look like child's play, and the two of you probably won't want to ask that handyman who lives next door to help you out on this one. It could even be dangerous. One belt lets go and your valentine could be flung completely off the premises.

A whole store catering to the romantically challenged has

opened near my house, called the Rowe-Manse Emporium. It carries cards and candy and flowers and romantic CDs, but a guy like me can still get confused because the store also carries practical items someone like myself might mistakenly think were romantic, like kitchen splatter screens. "Keeps the grease off her, don't it?"

I was in unfamiliar territory here and didn't want to take a chance. I needed something that really said "I Love You" and I found a little something, a little package with hearts on the front and the very words "I Love You." It was a bag of "vacuum cleaner freshener" and I thought she'd just love it.

If you do *nothing* else, fellow clods, buy a valentine. I know, I know. You are a man, and you believe as I do that Valentine's Day and Mother's Day are creations of the greeting-card industry and you don't want to knuckle under. But this time you must. To buy nothing on Valentine's Day is to pay the dearest price of all. And don't wait until five till six for them to be marked down. A valentine stamped "35% Off" loses something. And sometimes all that's left are the "Happy Valentine's Day to a Swell Stepson."

Avoid: "To a Real Pal" and "To a Close Friend." I always go with something that has some *size* to it. Call me softhearted, but I always get the biggest valentine Kmart has in stock. And *sign* the card, will you? Sure, sure, "Sincerely" is fine.

How can a man who's been married twenty-five years continue to be, or at least act, somewhat romantic? I paid a visit to Greg Godek, self-professed "Mr. Romance," a guy who writes books about how to be romantic, holds romance seminars, creates romance software.

He thinks manly men are afraid of romance. He says, "Here's what goes on in a lot of guys' heads: if I buy her one rose today she's gonna want a dozen next month and the next month she's gonna want pearls." Ah, yes, the slippery-slope theory of romance.

Also, I point out, if I start bringing home candy and flowers all the time I'll make other husbands look bad and they'll think I betrayed the male species and that I'm possibly even . . . pussy-whipped.

Mr. Romance says to start thinking about romance selfishly if need be: "Do you want your partner to nag you less? Would you like to have sex more often? Would you like it to be better? Just be more romantic!"

Flowers and chocolates? "Flowers and chocolates," he says disparagingly, "are what I call generic romance. Be creative."

He brings his wife a gift almost every day! Underwear with red hearts on them; a street sign bearing their names; heart-shaped sunglasses; heart-shaped lollipops.

His book is *1001 Ways to Be Romantic*. A thousand and one! Naturally, some seem a little sketchy.

Number 498 is "Kidnap Her," as in grabbing her, blindfolding her, maybe tying her hands and not telling her where you're going. Now if most guys I know had their wives in that position they'd probably get rid of them somewhere, not take them out to dinner. Anyway, I think that's a violation of federal law, so how about something a little less dramatic.

Wear a Tuxedo Home from Work. Hmmm. Could be mis-construed by her as my having lost my job and enrolled in bartenders school.

Number 952: Place Items Under Windshield Wiper of Car (e.g., a McDonald's coupon). 953—Vacuum Her Car.

I tell him I don't think I quite *get* it.

"Look," he says, holding up a scarf. "I found this scarf to match the label on this wine bottle." He wraps the scarf around the bottle, ties it, and hands it to his wife, Tracy.

A scarf to match the wine bottle? He is not one of us.

At Work

*I*ncreasingly, the elderly are being judged by their ability to perform rather than by their age. I hate that.

We have people at CBS, where I work, so old that they've not only *signed up* for the corporate organ donor program—they're already actively *giving*. You see the guys with the little coolers sitting in the CBS lobby.

Thanks to age discrimination suits, boomers are now free to work forever—and never retire! Free to not lie on the beach, fish, read, play golf, or travel the world. Hurrah!

And while working forever, we are free to not advance very far because the older guys who have the jobs we want won't leave and don't have to.

For purposes of age discrimination suits, "40 years of age or older" constitutes an "older worker." *That's* depressing. But at CBS, the cutoff for "older worker" is "deceased or better." At 65, Dan Rather is one of the Young Guns; at 50, they give me the child's portion in the CBS cafeteria. Some correspondents are still doing a fine job at 2×40, and about all those of us in waiting can do is surreptitiously put a little extra salt on their food when they're not looking, and maybe leave the forwarding addresses of our nursing homes of choice should something open up. Not that I'm bitter.

After all, the retirement age of 65 was set in the 1880s by Otto von Bismarck, who was asked to create the first pension plan in Europe. Otto, a businessman, thought 65 was a good age at which to allow people to stop working and start reaping benefits since life expectancy in Europe then was 45.

50 is supposed to be a time when you have more disposable income, except that more employers are now finding *you* more disposable and without income of any kind, disposable or otherwise. The Bureau of Labor Statistics reports that people 46–54 now have a far greater risk than the average worker of being laid off.

Downsizing. Outsourcing. Youthenasia. Thanks for your 25 years of loyal service, goodbye, and please don't be offended by the strip search on the way out. Say, is that one of our staplers in your pocket or are you just glad to be leaving? They can hire a person half your age to do your work for half as much and do it half as well which seems plenty good enough these days.

Some of my fellow workers color their hair and have face lifts to maintain a more youthful appearance. One had an eye and brow job, and when I saw him on the elevator the other day he was so permanently wide-eyed I thought he'd either been struck by lightning or I'd forgotten to put on my pants.

James Kennedy, publisher of *Executive Recruiter News*, calls such people "bionic executives" with their hairpieces, face lifts, bridgework, tummy tucks, elevator shoes, and makeup.

Some experts predict that boomers will have two, three, four, or five different *careers* before it's all over—that we'll be sitting in classrooms at age 80 learning new skills. If you do your homework, you can stay up and watch Lawrence Welk reruns.

You do get to feeling a little old at work sometimes. This sounds like something from Dickens' time, but I remember glue pots on the copydesk at the *Chicago Tribune*. We'd type our stories on *typewriters*, then the copy editors (one wore an eyeshade) would move things around and insert paragraphs by literally cutting the stories with scissors and *pasting* them back together—just 17 years ago.

My first encounter with a computer came at *The New York Times*, where on my first day (which, of course, was a night), some hotel or other in Vegas caught fire and the editor threw a bunch of wire copy on my desk and told me to write a story.

"But . . . I don't even know how to turn the computer *on*," I sputtered.

"Oh, right down there," he replied helpfully, then ran off. I typed the story, erasing the whole thing and starting completely over every time I made a mistake.

In TV you feel a little old just having *worked* at a newspaper. So . . . Gutenbergian. People don't read newspapers anymore. This is a very bad thing. (People serving on the O. J. jury said they never read any newspapers.) TV producers and (some) correspondents do read newspapers, however. That's where we get our story ideas and our opinions. (Increasingly and unfortunately, we are reading supermarket tabloid newspapers, however.) I used to get calls from TV producers all the time when I wrote for newspapers. I remember a call from one TV producer who asked me for telephone numbers for my sources on a story, then said, "That was an interesting story, if you ever write another good one will you call us?" I told her I had no current plans to write anything good.

I have now been in the business 25 years. At this stage, people at the office start to look at you like you're walking around with a silver tea service on your head.

I started at Libby's food company on Michigan Avenue in Chicago, where I worked in the advertising department writing responses to customer mail:

"Dear Mrs. Johnson,

Please accept our sincere apologies concerning the Libby's frozen french-cut green beans you purchased containing a thumb. It was an accident, we assure you, and not a new serving suggestion. Enclosed please find complimentary store coupons worth 50-cents off on your next three purchases."

Three 50-cent coupons in lieu of what today would be a $200 million damage suit, corporate bankruptcy, and the loss of 50,000 jobs.

I learned valuable lessons there, like how to sleep on the job. I would go out to lunch with advertising executives who indeed drank three martinis. This is not modern mythology. I would return, put my head down on my desk and fall asleep. This was not good since I had no office, just a desk out in the midst of 100 others.

My next job was army photographer in Vietnam. This was a bad job. I hear people complain about their working conditions, but here was a job where people actually *shot* at you in the workplace. Couldn't OSHA have stopped that war? I also learned that photographers have to lay their lives on the line, while correspondents dressed up in starched Abercrombie & Fitch fatigues and had cocktails in Saigon. I gravitated toward writing.

I applied for a job at *The Washington Post* at the same time

Bob Woodward applied for a job at the suburban section of the *Chicago Tribune*. Both of us were rejected as unqualified. He got my entry-level job at the *Post* on the Metro desk, and I got his at the *Tribune*'s suburban section. And while he was becoming one of the most famous reporters in history for Watergate, I was covering sewer bond referenda and debates that raged into the wee hours of a Tuesday evening over whether or not to put pimientos in the corn in the school cafeteria.

I was writing a new column in Chicago when I bumped into the late great columnist Mike Royko at a party. He was single and wearing a nice suit accessorized by two very attractive and very young women clinging to it. He had been overserved and grabbed me by the throat, saying: "This young bastard is trying to steal my job." I took it as a compliment that he even knew who I was. No one ever did steal his job; no one could ever replace him.

With Royko looking hale and hearty, I left Chicago for *The New York Times*, but only after an editor there said to me, "You know, Russell Baker's 57"—implying, you know, the legendary humorist might be about to retire, leaving an opening for a fella like yourself. Well, it's 17 years later and Russell Baker is *still* 57, and pretty soon I will be too. He still writes and looks distressingly well.

At 50, I tire of the commute, and so have joined the new trend of working at home whenever possible.

Working At Home is said to be The Trend of The Future, combining new Enlightened Employee Relations with the latest Galloping Technological Advances, allowing Millions of Americans to enjoy The Best of Both Worlds and Just Stay Home.

Not all of us, yet. You can't stay home and make *molten steel* on the stove. It would play hell with the countertops. But, hey, leave all that stuff to the Japanese and the Koreans. We'll be at home, if you need us, in the Home Office, processing, trading, investing, consulting, and writing—using personal computers, home copiers, home fax machines, answering machines, and microwave ovens (for power lunches).

Work has always been a chore. Getting there has always been worse. By the time we get to work we suffer from combat fatigue. The New Age worker telecommutes from his electronic cottage. It takes but nanoseconds, and requires no subway tokens or embarrassing galoshes.

I work at home as often as I can. A touch of self-discipline is all that's required, which for some of us is a lot.

With the more than two hours a day I save by not commuting, I have time to read the paper thoroughly and to watch Geraldo and Regis Philbin—making *me* a better-informed employee. And spending more time with the kids makes me a *happier* employee.

My commute? Just up a flight of steps to the Home Office in the attic, where I turn on my computer and prepare to fill the blank screen with prose. I turn on all systems: computer, fax machine, printer.

Federal Express delivers things to my home faster than inter-office mail delivers down the hall. FedEx and UPS deliver my neighbors' things, too, since I'm here to sign for them while they're at work in Hopelessly Outmoded Conventional Office Building Work Environments.

Working at home means there is someone here to field important phone calls that might otherwise go unanswered. *"Hello, Jersey Brickface? No, I don't think we need any polyvinyl brick-like sheet goods for the front of our home today, thanks."*

I'm also here to answer the door: *"Oh, hi Carol. No Jody's not home. She's at the office until about seven. Then how about me as a fourth for bridge tomorrow at Martha Neal's?"* The audacity! I'm at home, so how busy can I be? Is that it?

Working At Home means every day is Dress Down Friday— I can always wear leisure wear, although I do find that sometimes getting out of my pajamas makes it easier to buckle down. The Home Office Worker should watch out for serious lapses in personal hygiene. Occasionally laundering that plaid flannel shirt can be essential to maintaining a modicum of self-esteem—not to mention your marriage.

That was my wife calling to ask if I'd mind taking a moment out from my workday to put a couple loads of dirty laundry in the washer—since she's: At The Office.

Time for lunch. No more of that hopping over to the Four Seasons for working lunches, which strain the pocketbook and hack away at productivity. You feel good about that as you dine on Skippy and Welch's on Wonder. Who's hungry anyway? When you work at home, the refrigerator is your constant companion.

I take a moment or two out to catch *The Young and the Restless* and *As (As the World Turns)*.

It's better now that the kids are in school. My infant daughter once answered the phone "Goo-goo, Gaa-gaa," when Lee Iacocca's office called back about my request for an interview. His office seemed reluctant to grant it.

Jersey Brickface is on the line again, apparently thinking my imitation brickface needs might have changed since this morning. *"No!" I snapped, "but would you like to chat?"* You can start to get a little lonely, Working At Home.

I bring in the mail. There is a new *Victoria's Secret* catalogue, which I quickly toss in the trash, fearing an incident that would cause me to sue myself for sexual harassment in the workplace.

On the way back to the attic office, I pass my bedroom, and since I always feel a little woozy after lunch, I take time out from my workday to lie down for a moment and rest my eyes, recharging the old batteries to make me an even *more* productive employee later in the afternoon.

I put the clothes in the dryer (Maybe I should start taking in ironing, too!), then I'm off to pick up my daughter at school. I like to get there a little early to chat with the other mothers. *"We're going to a designer outlet sale tomorrow,"* one of them says to me. *"I think they have a men's department. Why don't you come along?"*

"Love to," I say. *"Can't. Bridge at Martha Neal's."*

For years my routine would go something like this: drive daughter to gymnastics, son to basketball, pick up daughter at gym take her to violin, pick up son take to friend's house, pick up daughter, bring home, rotate tires, pick up son, bring home.

Six P.M. Wife calls, saying she's running a bit late and asking if I'd start cooking dinner. She has a taste for braised shoulder of lamb with glazed asparagus.

Seven P.M. I go up to the home office in the attic where my daughter has shut off the computer, explaining: "There wasn't anything on the screen."

"Shut up," I reply.

"Middlessence" or "Pre-Deceased"?

*I*t's not just the AARP letter from Deets. All of your mail starts to change when you depart that prime 18–49 age group. Instead of junk mail from Herman's World of Sports and Club Med, you start receiving offers from retirement communities—and cemeteries!

I'm holding a colorful brochure that just arrived from the Garden of Memories.

The Garden is pushing its nonsectarian mausoleum: "Aboveground burial. The clean burial. Isn't that the way you and your family want to be remembered? Does the thought of belowground burial disturb you?"

Right now, your f——ing-a right it does! I'm only fifty. How many people do you know who died in their fifties?

Wait. Don't answer that.

My favorite line in the Garden of Memories brochure reads: "ACT NOW AND GET 40% OFF."

Act *now*?!

Welllll, it *is* forty percent.

The Garden of Memories brochure goes on: "If you ACT NOW you'll no longer be disturbed by the thought of belowground burial" (*Or Anything Else*). "Why leave the choice of burial up to to the last minute when you may be in no condition to make the best decision?" (*Dead*).

Shortly after my fiftieth birthday I also received a nice brochure from a cemetery monument company. Discount tombstones! Tombstone outlet shopping! Wholesale!

It included a coupon worth $350 off on my next—next?—tombstone from the New Jersey Monument Company. $350! Makes you think. $350 off your stone, 40 percent off your plot. Starts to add up—if you ACT NOW!

The convincing tombstone brochure reads "please pay particular attention to the coupon as 'The Savings Are Legitimate.' " (Why the quotation marks around the "Legitimate" part?) The coupon offers $350 off on personal epitaphs such as "Beloved Father and Husband" or remembrance phrases such as "Always in Our Hearts."

"We are the only wholesale monument factory in New Jersey—ten minutes from Giants Stadium." Stop by after the game. Maybe that's where Jimmy Hoffa got his stone. He's supposedly buried in the end zone, you know.

"We are never undersold—never, never, never! We sell directly to the public for up to 50 percent LESS than you would pay at a MONUMENT DEALER. Call TOLL FREE for an in-your-home appointment. Visa and Mastercard.

"Free Double Design Upgrade." Dead, and still seeking upgrades.

Aging is a "privilege" enjoyed only by humans and a few pampered domestic animals like Randy, Peaches, and Scooter (our cats). Most creatures succumb to injury, disease, or predators, as seen in disgusting detail every night on cable TV.

We should probably all be dead by now. In 1900 the average life expectancy was forty-seven! Just 3 percent of the U.S. population lived past the age of sixty-five. Today, through the miracle of modern science, our life expectancy is seventy-five and biogenetically engineered tomatoes last forever.

You can't really blame these proactive entrepreneurs at the Garden of Memories for their direct-mail campaigns. After all, Dropping Dead is an activity people in their fifties are getting involved in—

It can be annoying and inconvenient. "I was at a funeral in Florida," complains Reuben, a colleague, "and Charlie was supposed to be installing video editing equipment for me while I was down there. I got back and nothing was done. He'd been delaying and delaying—you know how these construction people are—and I just blew up. I called his office and asked to speak to Charlie and they said I couldn't so I screamed about all the delays and said I wanted Charlie's ass over here right away. And that's when they told me: 'Charlie's dead.' It sounded like another excuse. How could he be dead? He wasn't old enough to be dead." Reuben was so taken aback he forgot to ask who would be handling Charlie's work while he was dead.

With the aging of America, how long till some entrepreneur opens the Drop Dead Shoppe, offering all your funereal needs: sympathy cards, flowers, death notices, mourning-attire boutique, caskets, eulogies, ministers, music, monuments, and advice on topics like padding that obituary: "Mr. Geist was twice the first runner-up for the Nobel Prize for Physics . . ."

There are already funeral homes with drive-through windows. I saw one in Pensacola, Florida—the Junior Funeral Home, Mr. Willie Junior, proprietor. An open casket is placed in a drive-through window where motorists pay their drive-by respects. "People want convenience," Mr. Junior said. "The deceased's friends can come by even when we're closed."

And there are outfits offering burial in outer space. Very new, very now, *verrry* aboveground. Celestis, Inc., of Houston (NASA's hometown) orbited Timothy Leary's ashes this year.

I stopped by one day to see Rafael Ross, who was selling the idea of alternative interment in outer space from his World Trade Center office way up in the clouds.

He said he already had some "cremains"—cremated remains—right there at the office awaiting the first liftoff, including those of an Italian woman and her cat, which were to go up together as one payload. Each launch would carry about seven hundred individual containers of cremains.

All "passengers"—as he calls them, in the grand tradition of funerary euphemisms—were to be sterilized with gamma rays, then hermetically sealed and vacuum-packed in ultralight, ultrastrong Torlon containers.

He anticipated very few, if any, uncremated passengers, explaining: "We charge by the pound," about ten thousand dollars a pound. The payload of the average cremated passenger will be about four pounds, although the bereaved has the option of orbiting as little as one pound of the loved one's ashes.

"We offer a choice of three trajectories," said Mr. Ross, leafing through promotional material headlined "Send Your Loved Ones to SPACE" and ignoring for the moment the torrent of calls and letters from people who think he is crazy, irreverently tampering with the heavens, and cluttering up the universe.

But there are also those callers who absolutely cannot wait to blast off. "They're excited about it," said Mr. Ross, "although they will be dead." Some tell him that they want to be in the heavens "closer to God," or "back where we all came from." Others say that they are simply too claustrophobic to be in a closed coffin, and still others can't stand the thought of worms.

"We have the 1,900-mile-up polar orbit," explained Mr. Ross, "the 22,300-mile geosynchronic orbit, and then our deluxe trajectory into deep space."

He hopped up and was out the door to continue spreading the word, hurtling across New Jersey in his Oldsmobile Rocket 88 to address a meeting of the Eastern Pennsylvania Funeral Directors Association, in Easton.

"Physicists project that the capsules orbiting at 1,900 miles will remain unchanged for sixty-three million years," he said in the car. "Space is the perfect resting place, absolutely peaceful and cold enough to preserve things forever. This permanence is a big selling point.

"Our deep-space shots will follow Pioneer 10 out beyond our solar system," he said in reverential tones. "Can you fathom that?" He admitted it was difficult to fathom, lost as he was at the moment in New Jersey.

"This may fly in New York," said one of the Pennsylvania undertakers, after hearing out Mr. Ross in Easton, "but people here are different. You offer the bereaved out here a space shot and you might quite possibly get punched in the mouth."

Others were hesitant about writing off the idea. "I would consider offering it to someone pre-need," said Jeffrey Naugle, another undertaker, "but it would seem inappropriate to bring it up in an at-need situation."

"If the price came down some people might be interested," said Mr. Naugle, noting that it is not as if they don't get some unusual requests as it is. "One of my families asked that cremains be scattered over town," he recalled. "I didn't think much of that idea. You know, people hang out their wash."

The undertakers asked about the legal and religious ramifications. One of them said: "Catholics are only to be cremated for good reason." Hollered another undertaker, "Ten thousand dollars a pound is a heckuva good reason!"

With that, they all repaired to the bar, where a local casket company was sponsoring a cocktail hour.

"People come out here from New York with the darnedest notions," said one of the dark-suited funeral directors, who spoke gravely with his hands folded at his belt buckle. "But in this day and age you never know. Best not to laugh at anything"—and he looked as though perhaps he never had.

It seems like more and more people *are* dead these days, doesn't it? It used to be just my grandfather. They say by this age you know more people in the obituaries than you do in the wedding and birth announcements (but, then, how *would* you know newborns?).

A fiftyish friend received a notice in the mail for the grand opening of a funeral home. He was offended and did not attend, but it sounded like a festive Sunday afternoon, so I did.

It was a dreary, chilly day, perfect for the occasion, the grand opening of the new Hallowell and James funeral parlor. Who would go to such a thing? More than three hundred people showed up.

I was greeted at the front door by none other than Harry James, who had laid to rest thousands, from bankers who wanted traditional, solemn services, to the biker who was buried in his motorcycle jacket after a service with electric guitars. He was justly proud of his new facility, which could accommodate two funerals or four wakes simultaneously.

I told Harry not to get too excited, that I was there strictly "pre-need." He gave me a free bottle of hand lotion plus a Hallowell and James Funeral Home sticker, which you place right on your phone in case you have the infirm over a lot.

Guests munched finger sandwiches (from the caterer, not the back room, he assured me) as they strolled through the showroom looking at the latest in vaults, like the Triune SST, and feeling the comfort of the caskets with Simmons Beautyrest mattresses and springs.

They sipped a (blood) red punch ("From the caterer," Harry swears) while admiring the thoroughly modern embalming room. "Fortunately," Harry explains, "there were no clients in here today. We had three this week before we officially opened." To Harry, it seemed a good omen.

I asked him if he thought it wise to open a facility here, in a rather transient suburban area where people don't have roots and where most residents aren't all that old.

"People today want convenience," Harry says. Dead people? "They don't want to return to their original hometowns or old neighborhoods even to be buried.

"We find a lot of elderly parents living out here with their children," he says, "and moreover it isn't just the old who are dying anymore. With all the stress and pressure today, many more younger men—and women—are dying than did ten or twenty years ago."

Harry noted that an industry trade magazine called *The American Funeral Director* reports that considering these factors and an apparent bottoming out of the death-rate decline, there is reason for "cautious optimism."

The
Life Extension
Institute

I am sitting in the waiting room at the Life Extension Institute in Palm Springs, California—waiting. Waiting to see a doctor, reading his back issues of *Golf Digest* and *Urology Today*, and thinking he probably pays next to nothing for them because he can subscribe for *centuries* at a time!

Why not take advantage of the substantial per-copy savings when you buy fifty-two hundred issues of *Time?* After all, the Institute is telling people it may well be able to extend their lives to 150 years! *Human*, not dog.

I look around the waiting room. That guy over there, he's probably 137 years old, for all I know. And that cute young thing he's with, couldn't be more than one-ten.

Waiting and waiting, but it's no big deal, now that we have all the time in the world. Maybe I should have waited until I was more mature to get married (105) and to start a family (120).

Finally, the receptionist calls me and I'm ushered into an examining room, which looks not at all like Boris Karloff's basement lab, as I had feared, but normal: the cotton swabs, the examining table, the complimentary paper dressing gown (which I forgo, being concerned about paper cuts and where they might occur).

I worry that the doctor will look like Boris himself, but when the door opens, in bursts a youthful, handsome, vivacious doctor more on the order of TV's Dr. Steve—Marcus Welby's former protégé, now dating Barbra Streisand. (It must be disheartening to Jewish girls everywhere that Barbra herself couldn't land a real doctor.)

This doctor, Dr. Neal Rouzier, looks real enough, dressed in a white lab coat, and accessorized with a stethoscope.

Dr. Rouzier—"call me Neal"—chats for a while, then begins sizing me up:

"You're fifty, you can't do what you used to do. You have no energy, chronic middle-age fatigue syndrome, no endurance, memory failures, no libido. How is your libido?"

I can't recall, so he continues, "You have some increase in centrifugal fat around the hips and abdomen. . . ."

Jesus! He started off like Marcus Welby, but he's now starting to sound like Don Rickles!

He taps my knee with a hammer: "Your coordination is decreased."

Then he goes for the jugular with both hands: "You have redundant tissue in the neck."

I've had enough. "Doctor," I say, "do your patients ever just slap you for all these insults?"

He backs off a step and says cheerily: "But this can all be reversed! Aging is simply a disease! And with any other disease we treat it! With hormone replacement therapy!" (And I'm not using too many exclamation marks. Dr. Neal is a fanatic!)

He prescribed more mysterious ingredients than you see on the side of a Spam can: HGH (human growth hormone), dehydroepiandrosterone (DHEA), melatonin, testosterone, progesterone, thymic hormone, thyroid hormone, and pregmenolone.

These, he claims, will bring about profound improvements in my energy, endurance, sex drive, memory, hair color, skin, upper-body definition, and my gut. Another Southern California doctor, taking HGH himself, claims it has allowed him to throw away his eyeglasses. Sounds like tent-meeting stuff to me. Heal! In the name of hormones!

Dr. Rouzier, like Sy Sperling at the Hair Club For Men, is not only a bigwig (so to speak) at the Institute, but "also a client," as Sy would say—a testosterone-smearing, DHEA-devouring, HGH-injecting son of a gun. He's only forty-four, with no plans ever to look fifty.

Some people come to the Institute wanting to start treatment in their thirties. It is close to Hollywood, and—it was pointed out—a short walk from the airport, which conjures the vision of hordes of the lame and halt limping toward the Institute as the already-cured sprint the other way to make their flights. The Lourdes of Palm Springs. I did witness one woman trying to cross the street to the Life Extension Institute when she was almost run over (Life Contraction!) by one of the many geezer motorists who ply the streets of Palm Springs blissfully unaware of traffic-control devices.

Dr. Rouzier says one thousand patient-clients are on the hormone-replacement program. Ron Fortner is one. Ron calls Palm Springs "God's waiting room," and says it's the ideal location for the Institute, what with the city's combination of money, age (Thrifty Drugs has a clearly marked "Incontinence" aisle), and California's special emphasis on youth and attractiveness.

Dr. Rouzier, whose own exercise regimen includes running

up ten flights of stairs a day (not easy in low-rise Palm Springs), doesn't mind gloating a little.

"I don't watch what I eat," he scoffs, "because it burns off." *Burns Off!* And not while you're participating in a triathalon either, but just while you're sitting there. Just like those somehow skinny teenagers you see watching TV, guzzling Big Behemoth Beverage sodas from the 7-Eleven and eating lawn-and-leaf-sized bags of nacho cheese chips.

Their secret is youth and Dr. Rouzier says he can have it FedEx'd to your door. The cost for everything runs maybe $350 per week, about $300 of that for the HGH, which you can't get just anywhere. You can get it from the pituitary glands of cadavers, but FedEx is better. It can now be made synthetically through recombinant DNA procedures, but is regulated by the FDA for use only by prescription and only in research. So, I would be a guinea pig. The Institute is allowed to prescribe HGH because it shares results achieved by patients with the Wisconsin College of Medicine—a research deal worked out by the Institute's founder, Dr. Edmund Chein.

Dr. Chein is not in today. Golf? No, he was serving a three-year probation sentence imposed by the California Medical Board for ethical violations that include false advertising and failing to share insurance moneys with doctors who provided care to his patients, among others. Dr. Chein testified in the Rodney King trial, misrepresenting himself as an orthopedic surgeon, which he is not, and a graduate of Cornell Medical College, which he is also not, having matriculated at the American University of the Caribbean Medical College. (No, his major was not "Tanning.")

Dr. Chein believes HGH may well cure diabetes, arthritis, heart disease, and cancer. He believes the government restricts the use of HGH because if everyone started taking it and living to be 150, government programs like Medicare would be crippled.

The FDA thinks much more research is needed on long-term effects of HGH. The Institute does not. "In time," says Dr. Rouzier, "their studies will be done and in twenty years I will be happy to run fifty miles to their funerals and present them with data that it really does work."

On the way out, Dr. Neal introduces me to a couple on the program: George and Kathy Pickett. Kathy is forty-nine, fast approaching fifty, and George is sixty-five, trying to back into it.

They show me a photograph of themselves relaxing at home in their chemically-enhanced bodies. Only a California couple would have such a photo: the two of them in skimpy bathing suits posing on a little pedestal in their living room—the kind of arms-raised pose a male-female trapeze act strikes after completing their performance. They look good in the photograph. I'm never sure, though, if people look good in photos because they're sucking it up and standing at just the right angle and have just thrown away the twenty-three bad prints or what, but this couple did look good.

They had Before and After photos. The Before pictures were not a pretty thing to see. It appeared over time that Kathy's stomach was in fact being EATEN AWAY, and that his chest was much better defined. (Mine is defined too; I would define it as "somewhat repulsive.")

"It really is true you can turn back time," Kathy gushes.

"I used to actually shuffle around the house," says George, hopping on a treadmill. "And my sex drive is greatly improved. You've got to make sure you're both on the same program because you'll drive her nuts chasing her around."

"Absolutely!" Kathy agrees. They make it sound like it would be tough to hold down a job.

Ron Fortner:
All-out Warfare in
the Attack on Aging

Ron Fortner is doing it all—everything known and not quite known to science—to fend off aging. And, frankly, he's starting to scare me a little, like one of those new biogenetically engineered tomatoes.

Ron seems normal enough, with human birth parents and everything, but he is really no longer like the rest of us.

"I have stopped aging," he proudly proclaims. Just like the damned tomatoes!

What Norman Schwarzkopf did to Saddam Hussein, Ron Fortner is doing to Father Time. At fifty, in male menopause, Ron drew a line in the sands of time, proclaimed "this far, and no farther," then launched an all-out attack on aging employing chemical and biological warfare.

Ron had the quintuple bypass right after his fiftieth-birthday party, then headed for one of the multitudinous cosmetic surgery centers scattered along the byways of Palm Springs like so many pay phones. They really should put up little signs for Cosmetic Surgery Stops like they do for public phones and rest rooms—those universal-symbol signs with no words, in this case showing smiley faces and crossed scalpels. Or maybe just pictures of Cher.

Some of the surgery centers there already have colorful plastic signs out front to attract motorists—signs that sort of look like the little ones for Wendy's—and one wonders if they might actually be cosmetic-surgery franchises with drive-through facilities:

"Welcome to Scalpel King, may I take your order?"

"I'll have the Big Gulp Gut Buster Lipo-Suck Deluxe."

"Honey-mustard gas anesthetic with that?"

"Please."

"That will be $1,995 for two minutes on our Ab-Vac 2000. Please drive up. Unbutton your slacks and make sure your car is in park during the procedure. Thank you."

It wasn't quite that easy, but Ron had the abdominal liposuction and face-lift combo, which is nothing out of the ordinary in Palm Springs, where plastic surgery is considered almost a civic responsibility, like mowing your lawn. Keeps the place nice. "Had my jowls removed too," Ron explains. "I used to have a turkey neck; a good stiff breeze and I became airborne."

Standing beneath desert palms, Ron is telling me something about someplace in the South Pacific where the natives climb up palm trees and ritualistically bombard their elders with big coconuts, and how he has no intention of ever letting anything like that happen to him. No wonder Ron is going to such great lengths.

Ron is wearing all black, to look slimmer, hipper, younger. And he drives a Midlife-Crisis-Mobile, a red convertible (which doesn't necessarily mean anything, because so do I).

He has begun exercising regularly on stationary cycles,

treadmills, and other devices that take you on tortuous trips to nowhere. I know. I watched him myself.

And he's eating right. Where Ron used to eat, like, deep-fat-fried killer whale blubber sandwiches on big buttered buns (with the large fries), now he consumes fresh fruits and vegetables and expensive bottled waters and health-giving blender drinks.

I didn't even know there were nonalcoholic blender drinks till I met Ron. Interesting. Ron pours some skim milk in there and fruit juice and throws in some wheat germ and fresh fruit and God-knows-what-else, mixes it up, and chugs it. I don't see it replacing the margarita.

But Ron goes way beyond diet and exercise. Next, he stands there in his kitchen and starts popping pills like popcorn, and trying to explain what they all are between pops and gulps of water: "all purpose vitamins" . . . "slow release niacin" . . . glug-glug . . . "antioxidants" . . . "DHEA" . . . glug . . . "the magic elixir of longevity" . . . "PC95" . . . glug-glug . . . "pharmaceutical grape-seed extract" . . . "ester vitamin C" . . . glug . . . "this fortifies your immune system" . . . glug-glug . . . "attacks free radicals in your body."

Free radicals? In my body? Well, sometimes I do feel like Abbie Hoffman is burning a flag in my duodenum.

After chugging the longevity cocktail and devouring a couple jars of pills, Ron repairs to the bathroom to rub testosterone gel on his balls. A fun alternative to the transdermal shoulder patch, I'd imagine.

At night, Ron does worse things than that in his bathroom. And, haven't we all? He takes a heavy dose of melatonin for a deep sleep, then sits on the commode and injects himself in the thigh with HGH, human growth hormone—because, Ron says,

Adult Growth Hormone Deficiency Syndrome is rampant in our society. (Outside the NBA.)

Told you it was an all-out attack. "I am not a lunatic," Ron explains, sounding a bit like that other Southern California guy who said "I am not a crook."

To naysayers, who think that he and other pill-popping pioneers really *are* lunatics, Ron has this to say: "I'd say the same thing Christopher Columbus said: 'The world is not flat, you won't fall off.' "

Human growth hormone doesn't make Ron really tall, as you might have guessed, but he claims it does give him more energy, supple skin, a leaner body, more lustrous hair, better memory, improved vision—and it eats the fat from his midsection. *Eats the fat!* Like battery acid. Or so he says.

"My sex drive has never been better," says Ron. "My wife would like a word with the doctor who is prescribing all this, and that word is 'Stop.' "

The HGH costs about three hundred dollars a week. But considering the number of explorers—guys like Ponce de León—who gave their lives seeking the fountain of youth, three hundred a week doesn't seem so bad. And Ron believes the fountain of youth is exactly what he's found.

He puts his convertible top down and fairly wafts to work on a perfect Palm Springs day, past palm trees and fountains, the bright sun reflecting off the gold medallion around his neck. He drives pretty passively, I observe, considering the testosterone gel.

"I'll easily live to be one hundred twenty," Ron is saying. But, Ron, who wants to be old for sixty years? "It won't be like that," he says. "I'll be in robust health, with hair and teeth and eyesight—and I'll be sexually active." With whom? What woman would have sex with a 120-year-old man, other than a 120-year-old woman, and who would have sex with her? I don't want to talk about it any more before breakfast.

"People have always just accepted aging as a fact of life," Ron says. "But it is not a fact of life. It's a disease, and I'm actively treating it. To arrest it, to ameliorate its symptoms, and, yes, to reverse it, is medically possible."

Reverse aging?!

Excuse me, is this the Sci-Fi Channel? Does reversing aging mean that if Ron mistakenly takes an HGH overdose, he could turn into a teenager and lose his driving privileges?

"I would like to be carded again once in my life," Ron says. "I'm tired of being asked if I want the senior-citizen discount, and tired of people looking at my seven-year-old son and saying what a lovely grandson I have."

He arrives at work, radio station KNS, and bounds up the flight of stairs to the studio. Ron tosses on a headset for his show, and tells listeners: "It is I, your devoted manservant, the formerly portly Prince of the Desert, now the Prime Minister of the Metamucil Generation." He can laugh about it now.

After the show, Ron looks me in the eye and boldly asks: "Look at me. How old do you think I am?"

"Ummm, honestly?"

"Yes."

I know how much this means to him, what with all the time and money he has in this project (Project Myself), so to be diplomatic I guess, "Forty-five?" But Boutros-Boutros Ghali I am not. Ron seems disappointed that I didn't guess, like, thirty-nine. Actually, I was thinking . . . oh . . . about fifty-four? Turns out he's fifty-five, but I didn't hear it from him.

P.S. I do hope you found this book
in the fiction section. I'm really 41.